MW00629549

Africa in the World

Africa in the World

Capitalism, Empire, Nation-State

FREDERICK COOPER

Harvard University Press

Cambridge, Massachusetts & London, England
2014

Library of Congress Cataloging-in-Publication Data

Cooper, Frederick, 1947– author.
Africa in the world : capitalism, empire, nation-state / Frederick Cooper.
pages cm
"The origins of this book lie in an invitation to deliver the McMillan-Stewart Lectures
at the W. E. B. Du Bois Institute of Harvard University. The three lectures that
became the book's core chapters were presented in February 2012."
Includes bibliographical references and index.
ISBN 978-0-674-28139-4
1. Africa—History—20th century. 2. Africa—Politics and government—20th century.
3. Africa—Foreign relations—20th century. 4. African diaspora. I. Title.
DT29.C59 2014
960.32—dc23
2013031634

Contents

Maps

Preface

The origins of this book lie in an invitation to deliver the McMillan-Stewart Lectures at the W. E. B. Du Bois Institute of Harvard University. The three lectures that became the book's core chapters were presented in February 2012. I am grateful to the Institute, and particularly to its Director, Henry Louis Gates, Jr., for giving me this honor and this opportunity. I am also grateful to Skip for asking the sharpest questions after each of my lectures. I would also like to thank Caroline Elkins, Emmanuel Akyeampong, and David Armitage for their generous introductions to the lectures and for presiding thoughtfully over each of them. The staff at the Du Bois Institute helped to make the experience an enjoyable one. The present text bene-fitted from questions from the audience and from a critique of the written version by Jane Burbank. Joyce Seltzer went beyond what most of us expect from an editor not only to provide encouragement and wise supervision of the publication project, but to give me a careful and astute reading of the text.

   In preparing the lectures for publication I have developed fuller discus-sions of several points that had to be compressed for the lecture format, rethought a number of points, and added references. But I have tried to keep something of the flavor of the original lectures. These are reflective essays, not a comprehensive analysis of Africa's place in the world. They are intended to increase the reader's thirst rather than to satisfy it. For me, they are a chance to look both forward and backward. I have been studying Africa long enough—I took my first course on Africa in 1967—to have followed repeated twists and turns of scholarship and the changing relationship of scholarship to events in Africa. The most important shift in scholars' perceptions of Africa was occurring as I began my studies: scholars and activists were trying to understand how the world had changed once colonial empires had given way to independent states, and they soon had to come to grips with the conflicts and disillusionment that followed independence. Among historians, the immediate urge was to prove that Africa did in fact have a history, that its societies were not caught up in the timeless continuities of "culture." They were concerned with providing a useful history, useful to the task that new states faced in convincing their citizens that they were on a common pathway toward progress.

As that path proved to be increasingly thorny, many scholars, historians among them, veered away from a stress on the authenticity of African experiences of history and toward a viewpoint that located elsewhere the determinants of Africa's fate. The story, in its different versions, became one of African dependence within a world economy rigged against it. Whereas in the late 1960s writing the history of European colonization was often seen as too much part of colonialism's own conceits, by the 1980s the need to understand how colonial rule shaped both institutions and patterns of thought and social relationships seemed inescapable. Interest in studying the colonial era became so strong that only a brave few stuck with earlier periods. Some historians sought a middle ground, sensitive both to Africa and to the world.

The initial focus of African history had been political, but it turned more economic and social, and then it became more centered on questions of culture. What Africans made of their changing situation came to be seen as at least as interesting as the ways social scientists could analyze what that situation was. There are now signs of a revival of interest in economic history and a revival of interest in Africa before colonization.

These shifts in perspectives occurred with my own adult lifespan. My initial interest in Africa reflected my naiveté as much as curiosity. As I was contemplating what to study as an undergraduate at Stanford University, the Vietnam war was becoming an acute political issue. I was reluctant to take up the study of southeast Asia because its fate seemed to me to be shaped by the violent American intervention. I did not want to focus on

Latin America because I thought it was trapped by its class structure. But from what little I knew about Africa, that continent seemed like a region of possibility—just emerged from the yoke of colonialism, with young, vigorous leadership, whose clear goal was social progress. African nations were proudly taking their place in the world. It took a few weeks of my first course to realize how far off my thinking was. That course was in political science, and in those days political scientists were less obsessed than they are today with testing universal models, and they actually studied politics in all its messy complexity. My first teacher, David Abernethy, was then a young assistant professor (although he seemed the font of experience and wisdom to me), and his careful research in Nigeria was helping to reveal the inadequacies of then-fashionable modernization theory to explain the politics of the continent. I soon learned that Africa's path to the future was not as open as I had assumed, that its past mattered a great deal, and that its relationship with the rest of the world was complex. In any case, I was on a trajectory I would never get off. I am still interested in the relationship of possibility and constraint in the study of African history, and I and other scholars still have a great deal to learn about how those possibilities and constraints play out in the past, present, and future.

The McMillan-Stewart lectures gave me a chance to revisit themes from past research and writing and to integrate them into current debates and subjects of inquiry that new generations of researchers have opened up. My earliest field work was conducted in coastal Kenya in the early 1970s and focused on the problem of slavery in the nineteenth century in a region shaped by close connections across the Indian Ocean and to the Arabian peninsula and, after mid-century, by increasing European intrusions. I continued to study questions of labor in East Africa, focusing first on agricultural labor on the coast after the abolition of slavery by the British colonial government, then on dockworkers in colonial Mombasa. After that, I ventured into a broad, comparative inquiry into the labor question in French and British Africa during the era of decolonization. That project took me to Senegal, to which I have been returning at various intervals over a twenty-five-year period. Along the way, I became increasingly aware that even doing a "microhistory"—say of a few thousand dockworkers in Mombasa—entailed understanding the actions of officials in London, for whom Mombasa was a tiny part of a big empire and who were reacting to strikes and demonstrations in the West Indies at the same time as events in Mombasa itself. Whereas my earlier project led me to theoretical work on capitalism and global economic connections, my more recent research pushed me toward comparative and theoretical analyses of colonialism and empire and toward collaborative projects with, most notably, Ann Stoler, Randall Packard, and Jane Burbank.

To study Africa in the world is to delve beyond what one scholar can accomplish, and the present book is deeply indebted to the work of many others, some of it cited in the endnotes, much of it the result of numerous conversations, seminars, and workshops over the years with African, American, European, Asian, and Latin American colleagues. Since I met Mamadou Diouf in Dakar in 1986, his insights in writing and conversation have shaped my understanding of francophone West Africa and its relationship to France and the rest of the world. My colleagues at the University of Michigan, where I taught for eighteen years, and at New York University, where I have been for the past eleven, might recognize some of their ideas in these pages.

Africa in the World

Introduction

In 1946 W. E. B. Du Bois published *The World and Africa: An Inquiry into the Part which Africa Has Played in World History*. He was recasting a book he had published in 1939, and the new circumstance gave added significance to his insistence that Africa's part in world history was and would continue to be important. Europe was in a catastrophic state; colonial business as usual would not be resumed. Here was an opportunity for Africans to redefine their place in the world. But the main topic of his book was what Africa had brought to world history. Du Bois looked back as far as ancient Egypt and Ethiopia to trace a long lineage of African accomplishment in state-building. He demonstrated as well the fruitfulness of African efforts at agricultural production and commercial exchange. African history had taken a decisive turn for the worse with the advent of the slave trade and then with colonial conquest and rule. But Du Bois's main message was that Africans had long experience of ruling themselves and could do so in the future.[1]

Du Bois wrote in the aftermath of a war that weakened winners as well as losers, particularly the two major colonizing powers in Africa, Britain and France. Now, almost seventy years later, it is illuminating to look again at the relationship of Africa to the world at the end of World War II, to consider the pathways that brought Africa to that juncture, and to explore the pathways to the future that appeared possible at that time, both those

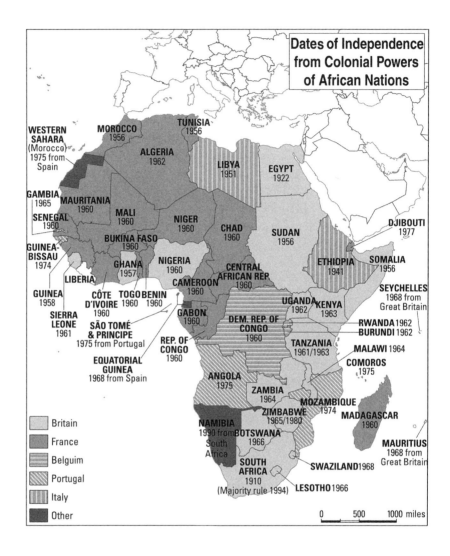

Dates of Independence from Colonial Powers of African Nations

WESTERN SAHARA (Morocco) 1975 from Spain

MOROCCO 1956

TUNISIA 1956

ALGERIA 1962

LIBYA 1951

EGYPT 1922

GAMBIA 1965

MAURITANIA 1960

SENEGAL 1960

MALI 1960

NIGER 1960

CHAD 1960

SUDAN 1956

DJIBOUTI 1977

GUINEA-BISSAU 1974

BUKINA FASO 1960

GHANA 1957

NIGERIA 1960

CENTRAL AFRICAN REP. 1960

ETHIOPIA 1941

SOMALIA 1956

LIBERIA

CAMEROON 1960

GUINEA 1958

CÔTE D'IVOIRE 1960

TOGO 1960

BENIN 1960

UGANDA 1962

KENYA 1963

SEYCHELLES 1968 from Great Britain

SIERRA LEONE 1961

SÃO TOMÉ & PRINCIPE 1975 from Portugal

GABON 1960

DEM. REP. OF CONGO 1960

RWANDA 1962

BURUNDI 1962

REP. OF CONGO 1960

TANZANIA 1961/1963

MALAWI 1964

EQUATORIAL GUINEA 1968 from Spain

COMOROS 1975

ANGOLA 1975

ZAMBIA 1964

ZIMBABWE 1965/1980

MOZAMBIQUE 1974

MADAGASCAR 1960

NAMIBIA 1990 from South Africa

BOTSWANA 1966

MAURITIUS 1968 from Great Britain

SOUTH AFRICA 1910 (Majority rule 1994)

SWAZILAND 1968

LESOTHO 1966

Britain
France
Belguim
Portugal
Italy
Other

0   500   1000 miles

that were taken and those that were not. I will explore ways to think about Africa's place in a world once dominated by European colonial empires and still shaped by capitalist economic relations. Du Bois recognized the importance of the post-World War II conjuncture, but he could not foresee how history would then unfold. What historical trajectories shaped the possibilities and limitations that Africa faced at that time? Why of the different pathways out of empire that African leaders envisioned in the 1940s and 1950s did the one ultimately followed lead to the nation-state, a political form whose dangers were recognized by influential African political leaders at the time? Will exploring the alternatives Africans faced and created for themselves in the past help us think more creatively about alternatives for the future?

Du Bois was not alone in thinking about Africa's place in the world. Other activist-scholars from the late 1930s and 1940s focused in insightful ways on the relation of Africa to capitalism and to empire. Behind these interventions was the question of liberation: how would Africa get out from the yoke to which it was bound and take up the place it merited in the world?

The conquest of most of Africa by European powers had taken place in a relatively recent past—the last third or so of the nineteenth century. At no point did colonial domination go uncontested, and not just by the leaders of indigenous communities defending themselves against encroachment. Africans educated in European-run schools turned assertions of the superiority of European civilization into claims that colonial regimes should live up to their stated principles of democracy and progress, and people of African descent in the Americas saw the connection between their own experience of racial discrimination and Africans' experience of colonial oppression and exploitation. For a time, colonial powers were able to contain the challenges that political connections within and beyond the African continent posed, taking advantage of the diversity and difficult communications that characterized the African continent and the fragmentation their own policies had induced. But in the late 1930s and then during World War II, the political situation was transformed, and social mobilization in Africa coincided with movements for liberation on a world scale.

Two events of the mid-1930s shook up the world of empire of which Africa was a part. One was the Italian invasion of Ethiopia in 1935, notable for its widely publicized brutality and the impotence of the other European powers in the face of a blatant act of aggression against a peaceful country with a long history of self-rule. The event galvanized political activists of African descent around the world, leading to the formation of political action committees on both sides of the Atlantic. The invasion made all too clear what colonization was really about, and many people in the African diaspora saw it as imperialism's assault on the black race—and the harbinger of the wave of conquest and racism that would soon engulf the world. The second event occurred in one of the oldest regions of European colonization, the Caribbean. Between 1935 and 1938 a series of strikes and riots irrupted in Barbados, Jamaica, Guyana, and other British territories. Officials, once they got beyond their initial tendency to attribute all disorder to the irrationality of backward peoples, came to realize that poverty and hopelessness lay behind the "disorders." So serious was the matter that the government cancelled the celebrations that were to be held in 1938 for the centenary of the last stage in the abolition of slavery in British colonies, something for which British officials were usually eager to claim credit. But now it appeared that a century of emancipation had left the descendants of slaves with little to show for the economic benefits of freedom. Strikes also broke out in a number of African minetowns and transportation centers, and the labor question began to look in London like a problem on an imperial scale.[2]

Then there were the ways in which world war was experienced by people of African descent around the world. It was in some ways a positive experience: Britain, and then the United States, needed the strength and the blood of all their peoples, and military service provided both material advantages and recognition, in British, American, and (for a brief period before their defeat) French armies. Africans and others took seriously the promise of the Atlantic Charter of August 1941 in which the leaders of Britain and the United States mounted a principled defense of self-government against the aggression of the Axis powers. Although British Prime Minister Winston Churchill seemed to think the words applied to white people only—and especially the victims of Nazi aggression in Europe—others took the words to be universal. As the war turned in favor of the Allies, Pan-African activists—coming out of networks that linked African and West Indian port cities to London, New York, and sometimes Moscow—felt themselves empowered. They knew how much their contribution to the war effort was needed, and they saw themselves as part of a worldwide struggle against tyranny.

That Europeans were killing each other, that Japan was showing it could defeat European armies in Southeast Asia, and that the war was, at one level, being fought for freedom and against racism made the ideological ramparts of colonial empire look increasingly fragile. The war years and the years immediately thereafter brought a new self-confidence to African liberation movements. This was the moment when African American political leadership went furthest in identifying its efforts to end discrimination and bring about full inclusion in American society with the quest of African movements for political voice, social equality, and economic betterment—all in the name of "400 million black people scattered around the globe. . . ."[3] It was in this context that Du Bois published *The World and Africa*.

His book joined others in making a double case for liberation: pointing to the importance of Africa and Africans in the making of the modern world and demonstrating the destructive effects of the slave trade and colonization on Africans. One of the pioneering and most enduring texts of the time was C. L. R. James's *Black Jacobins*, published in 1938.[4] It was written during the period of strikes and confrontations in the British West Indies between 1935 and 1938. For James, a Trinidadian, to write a book about the struggle for liberation of the slaves of Saint-Domingue between 1791 and 1804 was to point to the struggle for liberation that remained. For him, Haiti—emerging from the revolution as an independent republic—should have been in the vanguard of global liberation, but French, American, and British elites had sought instead to quarantine the Haitian revolution, to treat it as black mischief. By restoring the revolution to history, James was exhorting colonized people of his own era to see the possibilities of emancipation.

James's arguments grew out of a thorough and penetrating work of history. He did not regard plantation slavery as an outdated form of economic life, but—in all its brutality—an intrinsic part of capitalism. The discipline of the sugar fields stood alongside that of the textile mills of England as the founding elements of the capitalist economic system—and hence the starting point for the revolution to come. James underplayed the African elements in the revolution, notably the religious and cultural ties on which the largely African-born slave population drew to act collectively. He wanted his revolutionaries to be the heirs to the Jacobin tradition of the French revolution.[5] He described how Toussaint L'Ouverture, the great hero of the slave revolt, had sought liberation within as well as outside the colonial system; he was for a time a Commissioner of the French Republic. For James, the ultimate goal was the revolutionary transformation of the world, not the independence of individual territories. His book remains a compelling analysis of a slave economy and of a movement against it—a movement that drew on slaves, freed slaves, and gens de couleur (children of French fathers and slave or ex-slave mothers), sometimes working together, sometimes betraying each other. It was a social movement that was more than the response of a single category of people expressing its "identity." It was an effort that crossed social lines, with all the possibilities and limitations such a process entailed.[6]

In 1944, another Trinidadian, Eric Williams, published *Capitalism and Slavery,* like the *Black Jacobins* a treatment of the slave plantation as integral to the development of the modern capitalist economy. He argued that slavery accounted for much of the capital formation that made the industrial revolution in England possible and that Britain decided to abolish the slave trade when slavery was no longer profitable. Both these propositions, in their literal form, have been much criticized, but if the relationship of slavery to capitalist development was more complex than Williams admitted, the connection was vital nonetheless. Williams was a political activist, who later became Prime Minister of Trinidad. For him, analyzing the world was to change it, to step out of colonial capitalism, West Indies style, into new possibilities.[7]

Also in 1944, a white American, Melville Herskovits, widely regarded as the founding father of African studies in the United States and an anthropologist who worked on both sides of the South Atlantic, published an article in *Foreign Affairs* that made a direct linkage between African kingdoms like Dahomey, which he had studied, and the post-colonial future of Africa. African institutions, not just European models, could be the basis for modes of governance. I first ran across Herskovits's piece in the archives of the Government General of French West Africa. Top officials circulated the text to district administrators and demanded that each official write a response to it. Of course, they did not like Herskovits's article,[8] but the broader issue it raised—in the context of increasing activism on the part of African social and political movements—would soon open up the question of what alternative forms of government to colonial rule could be imagined.

Might not African notions of social and cultural life be combined with selected political ideas stemming from Europe—particularly the notions of rights and citizenship—to pose a realizable alternative to the oppressive, constricted colonial system and to capitalist exploitation? Such ideas were set forth at the Pan-African Conference in Manchester in 1945, the latest of a series of Pan-African conferences dating to 1900. Du Bois, then 73, as well as such future African leaders as Kwame Nkrumah and Jomo Kenyatta were present. But the resolutions of the Conference did not go far in specifying the institutional forms that liberation could take. The initiative after 1945 moved in a different direction, not least because France and Britain were sufficiently shaken to restructure their regimes and African leaders were ready to seize and widen the opening.

Notable in this regard was Léopold Sédar Senghor of Senegal, poet, onetime teacher in a French lycée, former prisoner of war in Germany, and leader of the négritude movement that had insisted throughout the 1930s on Africa's contribution to world civilization. In 1945 he contributed to a book with the revealing title *A French Imperial Community*. Senghor informed his French readers of the achievements of African civilizations, and he told his African readers, "assimilate, do not be assimilated." He meant that Africans should avoid either closing themselves in their own cultures or uncritically adopting European ways, but should fashion their own synthesis, thereby making a contribution to a universal civilization. For now, he was arguing for Africans to take their part in transforming empire from a structure of invidious distinction into a pluralistic community that conjugated equality and difference. Senghor, elected by Senegalese in the fall of 1945 to the assembly writing a new constitution for post-war France, would soon try to put those ideas into practice.[9]

Colonialism and capitalism, Senghor, Williams, James, and Du Bois all believed, reinforced each other. Senghor feared that "nominal" independence for small, poor, weak territories—the formal end of colonial rule without the capacities to govern effectively—would serve only to perpetuate poverty. The solution to the iniquities of colonialism and capitalism, for Senghor, was not to exit from empire but to transform it, not to withdraw from the world economy but to transform it too. Senghor's colleague in the constitution-writing assembly in Paris in 1946, Aimé Césaire, argued successfully for a fuller integration of the former slave islands of the Antilles into France, as departments with the same status as those of the metropole. Césaire's searing indictment—*Discours sur le colonialisme* (1950)—was a call for world revolution, not for secession or autarchy.[10]

Senghor's less revolutionary version of colonial emancipation focused on the relational character of world politics. He called for a combination of horizontal and vertical "solidarity": horizontal, of Africans with each other, the only way to acquire the political strength to challenge the colonial powers, and vertical, of French Africans with European France, a frank recognition of the realities of poverty, lack of infrastructure, low levels

of education and technical skills in Africa, and the value for Africa of
European notions of rights—all of which he insisted required turning the
French connection into something positive.

In the chapters that follow I look at Africa in relation to the world beyond
the continent, exploring not only the invidious entanglements of the slave
trade and colonization, but also the relationship of horizontal and vertical
solidarities, the possibilities they entailed, and the constraints they
encountered in the context of a history of capitalism and of empire. In
doing so, I hope to recapture the range of political imagination of the
1940s and 1950s, something occluded by our read-back of the patterns of
the 1960s as if they were the only way change could be imagined.
    Africa has been reimagined in different ways over the years—by intel-
lectuals and scholars inside and outside the continent, by journalists, by
young people making their way in an uncertain world, by political elites.
For scholars, the most important shift occurred as they came to grips with
the triumphs of African states' acquiring independence from colonial
rulers, with the continued struggles in those parts of Africa that remained
for decades longer under white domination, and with the conflicts and
disillusionment that followed independence. In the early days of African
studies, scholars in Europe and North America were acting, as John
Lonsdale astutely put it, like a "Committee of Concerned Scholars for a
Free Africa."[11] This perspective implied a focus on the independent nation-
state—as the objective of political movements leading up to independence
and the focus of political thinking and action afterward—as well as on
national development and national culture. Two events marked a crisis in
this way of thinking about Africa: the 1966 coup that overthrew Kwame
Nkrumah as ruler of Ghana and the Biafran war, beginning in earnest in
1967 as a part of Nigeria attempted to secede from the newly independent
state. The nation was not necessarily turning out to be the focus of unity
and common action.[12]
    If independence from colonial empire was not sufficient to set Africa on
a path to progress for most of its people, Du Bois's question about Africa's
relationship to the world had to be pondered anew. Nominal independence, some argued, left African countries with insufficient political and
economic clout to counter the machinations of the old colonizing powers—
or new "imperialist" powers like the US or the USSR—or to influence the
terms of interaction with the transnational corporations. Colonialism, in

such an argument, had simply given way to "neo-colonialism." Others wanted to push the story backward in time—to reveal the subordination of the "periphery" to the "core" of a capitalist world economy whose origins lay in the unequal way in which commercial exchange had taken place ever since the fifteenth or sixteenth centuries. Still others insisted that the trajectory of African economies—and the eventual political subordination of the continent—should be understood not so much in terms of commerce, but in terms of production, the confrontation of societies that harnessed land and labor in very different ways, leading to increasing vulnerability and impoverishment on one side and increasing wealth and military and political might on the other. Such considerations animated a radical reconsideration of African history in the 1970s and into the 1980s.

The problem with such ways of thinking about Africa in the world was that explanation was based on that which had to be explained—the unequal capacity to shape economic and political relationships. How did the relationship of Africa to Europe come to be so asymmetrical? Scholars have been too quick to leap from the unevenness of power, which reached an extreme in the nineteenth century, to an assumption that capitalism, Europe, or colonialism was necessarily an overwhelming force in the world. European dominance in turn became the reason for the different fates of the continents.

Yet assessing the power of European states to colonize and capitalist enterprises to exploit cannot begin with a simple assumption of dominance. Scholars have trouble conceptualizing asymmetrical relationships, which nonetheless do not imply total power of one side over the other. To explore such relationships is to see the limits of power as well as its extent and above all to look at how people on the weaker end of the connection pushed back. One should not simply look at such efforts as the heroism of resistance, but ask if such actions actually had effects—making total dominance too difficult or expensive, opening fissures in structures of power, opening niches in which some Africans, perhaps at the expense of others, could find advantage in relations with an imperial power and partially shape the nature of the interaction with that polity.

The "and" in Du Bois's *The World and Africa* points in two directions. African history should be studied in all its complexity, but not as if "Africa" existed independently of the rest of the world. The connections that influenced the course of African history go back deeply in time—before the development of capitalism, before European conquests on the continent.

These connections were part of the trajectory that *produced* capitalism. One can no more write world economic and political history properly without considering Africa than one can write African history as a pristinely indigenous story.

Analyzing the place of European colonial empires in African history forces us to confront the fact that empires, as vast political entities, had to make their power felt in particular contexts. Conquest was usually the easier part of empire building; administering an empire—let alone transforming societies—was the hard part, and most successful empires found ways to co-opt local elites into the crucial role of intermediary, a role that gave them at least some room to maneuver. Colonial empires in Africa—despite the extremes of technological advantage and racialized arrogance that they exhibited—were no exception, and imperial history, if it is to reflect the actual workings of empires, slides into African history.

Studying such a history of uneven and unequal connections poses challenges to the historian. Research in or about multiple sites takes time, money, languages, and mastery of different historical and geographical contexts. No individual can do research on all aspects of even a well-defined project in long-distance exchange, the movement of religious ideas, or the networks that anticolonial activists built up across the world. The ability to change focal length becomes essential: to zoom in on local actors and local forms of interaction in Africa, to zoom out to understand, for example, the ideological, administrative, and political baggage that imperial elites carried with them across an entire empire, the importance of mutual influence, cooperation, and rivalry among different empires, and the circulation of anticolonial activists from Accra to London to New York and to Moscow. The methods of oral history that specialists in African history have emphasized can be used to follow people as they moved, not just to get a full understanding of the localities they come from. Tracing connections in all their specificity can move us beyond an African history that looks inward on the continent and turns an otherwise amorphous notion of "the global" into an analysis of the mechanisms and limitations of interaction among continents and peoples.

1

〜o〜

Africa and Capitalism

Let us start out with Africa's place in the evolution of the world economy. Much writing on wealth and poverty tries to explain Europe's riches by virtue of its supposedly inherent characteristics: the scientific spirit, the Protestant ethic, openness to commerce, or a bent toward incremental technological innovation. Africa has served as a foil for such arguments: cultural predispositions that run against economic rationality, too strong kinship ties, weak notions of personal property, and—with twentieth and twenty-first century variations—a tendency toward personal, tyrannical, anti-entrepreneurial governance.[1]

The question of global economic divergence has been given a scholarly push out of static comparisons by Kenneth Pomeranz, historian of China, and Prasannan Parthasarathi, historian of India.[2] Part of Pomeranz's argument is a sophisticated revival of the Williams thesis. He claims that Britain—and especially its industrial regions—only pulled ahead of China economically around 1800. Britain's overseas empire put together in the seventeenth and eighteenth centuries was, he insists, critical to the industrial takeoff of the nineteenth. West Indian colonies, employing African slaves, enabled England to profit from complementarities in land and labor: without West Indian sugar supplying a large portion of the calories to workers in the mills, much land and labor in England would have been diverted to growing calorie-rich crops. Had slave-grown cotton from the southern United States not become cheaply available in the early nineteenth century the English textile industry might have had to draw on domestically grown fibers, again with high opportunity costs in land and labor. Pomeranz points to the "exceptional scale of the New World windfall, the exceptionally coercive aspects of colonization and the organization of production there, and the role of global dynamics in ensuring the success of European expansion in the Americas." Chinese empire, he claims, had no such complementarities—it extended over rice- and wheat-producing land that was part of the same system as the region with industrial potential. Within its own configuration of imperial ties and regional economic relations, China's producers (and government) followed perfectly rational strategies and accumulated considerable wealth, but they did not provide the same impetus to industrialization as did the combination of factors that provisioned Britain's version of empire.[3]

That England had a state apparatus capable of enforcing property rights, backing up employers' disciplining of labor, and protecting commerce is also an essential part of the story.[4] The growing capacity of the state in the eighteenth century was in turn conditioned by the imperial nature of that state—its need for fiscal and military resources to extend and maintain its reach into Ireland, the West Indies, North America, and India. Empire was making the British state, not the other way around.

Parthasarathi focuses on another dimension of imperial connections. As of the early eighteenth century, Indian cotton textiles were more desired in world markets than anything Britain could produce, but Britain was able to use its central point in imperial networks to become a relay station between Indian producers and markets. A key link here was, once again, the slave trade: Indian textiles, via Britain, went to Africa to pay for slaves who ended up in the Caribbean helping to grow sugar, enhancing the buying capacity of Euro-Americans, who bought more cloth. British manufacturers were under pressure to innovate to counter Indian dominance of production, and they were aided by a government willing to impose tariffs and other barriers to protect a developing industry. The imperial state—with its navy and its effort to concentrate economic power—was able to enforce the tariffs and commercial regulations (the Navigation Acts) that kept Dutch and other trading competitors at a disadvantage. Yet another dimension of imperial power came into play by the early nineteenth century: British control over India was sufficient to ensure that

Indian industrialists would have no comparable help in keeping up with innovations. India went from industrial exporter to exporter of primary products.

Both explanations posit Britain's divergence as a kind of leapfrog. The Qing and Mughal empires were doing just fine as large-scale land empires, with governments that presided over commercially active societies and collected sufficient revenues to maintain and expand a large imperial apparatus while leaving considerable space to farmers, artisans, manufacturers, and merchants to operate. Britain, in a violently competitive European state system and in need of external resources, did the most advantageous thing it could: build a fiscal-military state, capable of sponsoring and protecting plantations overseas and factories at home. Its particular form of empire-building—militaristically and economically aggressive—came out of a necessity that the other great empires of the time, Qing, Mughal, or Ottoman, did not face. The "divergence" of the British economy reflected both its capacity—coercive, financial, economic—to concentrate resources and its capacity to prevent others from doing so, be it in the form of tariffs and commercial regulations deployed against European competitors, colonial controls in India, or naval power at sea. One might draw a different lesson from one frequently claimed as the source of European economic success and power, that is the miracle of the unfettered market. Rather, the fetters—imposed selectively—helped to produce the market. A relatively strong state was key to Britain's industrial takeoff, as arguably an activist state was to Asian "tigers" in the late twentieth century.[5]

One reason why the arguments of Pomeranz and Parthasarathi have attracted so much attention is that both scholars started out as historians of East and South Asia. They did not come to the project looking for a set of attributes of Britain—or Europe—that made it great. They came from a different direction and sought answers by looking at the shifting places of England, China, and India in interaction across space and by looking at "divergence" as a process, not an attribute—a process shaped by the exercise of imperial power.

What does all this have to say about Africa? Not that Africa, like China or India, stood on the edge of its own industrial development. The value of these arguments is in their focus on relationships, on the different positioning of political entities—kingdoms, empires—in relation to each other across interconnected spatial systems. It would be misleading to assert

Relations

that there is a normal pattern of economic growth—from which Africa deviates—or to invert the arguments of the Africa-bashers by considering Africa a mere victim. Africa's economic history is not that of continual backwardness, shared poverty, choking overpopulation, or unremitting subservience. Its history is also one of adaptation to difficult ecosystems, of trading systems that linked different producers across long distances. African entrepreneurs adapted—whether for better or for worse—to external demands for their products.

But questions remain about the forms innovation and adaptation have taken and the effects of adaptation, constraint, and resistance on connections to world markets. Much of what Africa is up against today—not least the denigrating terms in which its future is debated—is not a consequence of "failure" so much as of the partial success of a large number of its people in responding to—or staving off—efforts at economic domination, from within and abroad.

Africa's human geography—relatively low population, varied landscapes—provided many places to hide and few in which to build regimes of exploitation. The would-be king or the would-be employer of labor could attract or coerce followers—hence the high population densities near the Niger River or the East African lakes going back several centuries—but their efforts were constrained by the danger that organized groups of kinsmen could move elsewhere to establish their communities.[6] It was difficult for an elite to entrench itself by monopolizing control of land; doing so would have risked an exodus of would-be subjects and followers, whose service in many capacities—fighting, raising children, working—was the most valued resource. Land was hardly there for the taking, but access to it was in general mediated through kinship and village-level structures.[7]

For a would-be king or dominant class, enrichment via escalated exploitation of local people was a dangerous endeavor. Bringing in outsiders—slaves for example—was a more attractive option and a major factor in both Sahelian Africa and the coastal kingdoms of West Africa. Even in this regard, elites had to be careful. Studies of African slavery show how wary slaveowners were of locally born slaves, who had the connections and knowledge to organize collective flight or resistance. In most contexts, African slaveowners preferred to reproduce a slave labor force by integrating older or second-generation slaves and raiding for or buying new ones.[8]

The "exit" option, as Albert Hirschman calls it, was thus relatively open in much of Africa—including the near-hinterland of much of the Atlantic coast as well as the Sahel. Exit was a social possibility, resting on the strength and flexibility of kinship networks and other forms of affiliation. Exit of course changes the terms of other options—"loyalty" and "voice" in Hirschman's schema.[9] Not all parts of the world had such a viable exit option: geographic closures, higher population densities, and the relative weakness of corporate kinship groups made other regions more vulnerable to the exactions of would-be kings or would-be exploiters. Africa had a long history of statebuilding, but even as kinship groups in such situations were made to pay tribute, contribute fighting men, or agree to marriages that allowed the king to expand his lineage, the lineages could make kings accommodate to them and accept checks on authority.

Such considerations can help us understand the early interactions of West Africans with the first Europeans—from the Portuguese kingdom—who came to their shores in search of gold and slaves in the fifteenth century. At that time, coastal Senegambia and Guinea-Bissau were at the fringes of the great Mali empire. This empire (see Chapter 2) covered a vast area, and its power was based both on its coercive capacity and its ability to give local elites in many areas an interest in accommodation, thanks to its situation on the critical nodal points connecting the Sahelian region with North Africa across the Sahara desert.

These routes were of great importance, not just for the economic connections they forged between Africa, the Ottoman Empire, and the greater Mediterranean, but for their cultural and political impact.[10] As one would expect, Mali's rulers did not exercise tight control over its component parts, and it did not impose its own cultural patterns on all its subjects. Its elite was Muslim, and Islam often flourished in spaces crisscrossed by trade routes, and particularly among merchant diasporas. Mandinka traders spread from Mali across vast spaces of West Africa, including to the gold mines south of the Empire's center, but also to the southwest. Their presence gave rise to cosmopolitan communities, familiar with trade, operating in an ambiguous field where the power of kings was at times to be respected, at times to be kept at a distance.

Trade in slaves was part of what made these networks work. The strength of the economic system was not in the intensiveness with which slaves or anyone else could be exploited, but in the connections across space that elites could manage, networks forged out of trust reinforced by Islam as well as by interest. Toby Green argues that the experience of people in the Senegambia-Guinea region with such forms of commercial interaction in the Sahel and across the Sahara enabled them to adapt quickly and profitably to the arrival of Portuguese traders.[11]

The "Portuguese" presence in coastal West Africa derived from an equally particular route. Green points to the role of "new Christians," Portuguese Jews who were forced to convert in the early sixteenth century and then dispersed. A group of them established themselves in the Cabo Verde islands, seeking to trade in a variety of commodities and grow crops in a favorable tropical climate. The Cabo Verde traders developed a particular sort of community and a particular sort of trading system, adaptable to making contact in diverse environments and to forming commercial relationships with people who were not like themselves. Hardly intent on any world-spanning project of empire-building, they nonetheless put together connections that eventually gave rise, for a time, to a Portuguese-dominated network linking Africa, Iberia, and the New World. And out of the commodities that interested the Cabo Verde merchants the one that led to the most important breakthrough was slaves.

The early European presence in West Africa was far from potent; traders stuck to their enclaves—or offshore vessels—and made their deals. Green argues that cosmopolitan communities with many mixed-race and more culturally mixed people carrying on business developed around such enclaves. Networks expanded beyond those of the Cabo Verde traders and the Mandinka diaspora with whom they made contact in ports along the coast. None of the actors—the first generations of African and Portuguese traders included—could know what was going on at the other side of the Atlantic and how much the patterns that grew out of their experience would, over time, have fateful consequences. It was only later, as back-and-forth contact across the Atlantic developed, that traders, some of slave descent, came to know the nature of the system they had helped to create. By the seventeenth century, many of the most important traders in the West African ports—trading in a variety of commodities as well as slaves—were "Luso-African," most often the product of Portuguese-African sexual liaisons, although some Africans also acquired the linguistic and cultural skills to become part of such communities.[12]

The interest of these West African elites in managing connections with the external world helps to explain the continuities of the slave trade and the variations that developed as it extended to other regions of Africa. G. Ugo Nwokeji, writing on the Bay of Biafra, and John Thornton and Linda Hayward on West Central Africa also call attention to the interface of African and European networks that created a spiral of involvement, regional militarization, and in some places the creation of Creole Atlantic societies.[13] Adaptation also took the form of a variety of currencies that Jane Guyer describes as "interface" systems that facilitated Atlantic commerce.[14]

Together, we see a range of adaptations to the demand for slaves: from centralized kingdoms with the top-down authority that were strengthened by slave trading, to the Aro of southeastern Nigeria who could adapt profitably to the demand for slaves through a more network-like mechanism, to kingdoms of West Central Africa where connections and alliances with Portuguese enveloped the region in conflict and produced large numbers of slaves. The latter case, especially in Angola, entailed the most direct involvement of Europeans in slave catching, but they had to work through alliances with African leaders, who were themselves in the process of constructing rival polities. When Dutch slavers entered the picture, the overlap of two European powers and different African polities fighting for power and for slaves gave rise to an unstable situation—devastating for thousands of people caught up in the conflicts. Whether a state could, in a sustainable manner, establish its power over a region, raid for slaves beyond its borders, and commercialize slaves captured by others in the region or whether multi-sided conflict and instability reigned, slaves were being captured and sent to ports, where European slaving vessels came by and made their deals.

The participation of African elites in such structures was a response to what they could and could not do, what they could and could not control. In this context, it means little to say that Africans were enslaving other Africans. African elites were not acting as Africans—for such a designation only came to have meaning in the context of the Atlantic world itself—but as would-be kings, emperors, or chiefs trying to extend their authority in conditions where individuals and collectivities had alternatives to pursue. To some kings and merchants in the slave trade era, participating in the slave trade made sense because both the obtaining and the disciplining of slave labor occurred externally to their power base. They raided far afield and sold the people they captured, giving up the potential profits of exploiting labor directly along with the risks of doing so.[15] They obtained commodities that elites could distribute to followers, like cloth, iron bars that could be used to make tools and contribute to agricultural and other activities that took place alongside slave trading, and guns that gave temporary advantage to the political elites that had them until their neighbors caught up—leaving a more militarized politics in place.[16] The nefarious connections had complex consequences: one of them was the introduction into Africa of New World crops—cassava, maize—that came to be regarded as African staples and may have contributed to the capacity of growing states to feed a denser population.[17]

The difficulties of African rulers in systematically exploiting their populations *in situ* coincided with one of the ugliest and most central dimensions of Euro-American history from the sixteenth century onward—the voracious appetite for labor in places, notably the Caribbean sugar islands, where indigenous populations had been killed off and where people with choice in the matter did not want to go.[18] Some African rulers and communities refused to sell slaves at various times, but connections have their advantages. Once someone in the region got into the slave-trading business, its capacity to make war and stage raids was increased; the availability of weapons and trade goods—necessary to acquire followers— changed the nature of political competition.[19]

In the nineteenth century, after the European change of heart on the slave trade under the impetus of abolitionist movements, African polities that had profited from such commerce had to make a transition from exporting to using slave labor. The shift was manageable in part because slave-trading kingdoms had never been exclusively slave-trading kingdoms; production and commerce were more complex and varied. Some nineteenth-century societies were quite successful in increasing the productive use of slaves. Faced with the continued problem of escape and the dangers of a slave class building up over generations, most slaveowners cycled captives through the status of slavery and, at least in second or subsequent generations, into positions of lesser subordination, at the cost of terrible slave raiding for new slaves to keep the system going.[20] European buyers of palm oil, cloves, or other African-produced commodities did not, at least for a time, have to ask questions about how the palm oil or cloves that they wanted were produced.

What is really the peculiar institution—despite the success of anti-slavery ideologues to attach the label the other way around—is capitalism, not just in the sense of commodity markets but above all in the organization of labor. The great divergence of the eighteenth century—in relation to China, India, or Africa—was not just a matter of an imperial state shaping Britain's relation to world markets, but a transformation of labor relations at home.

Here Marx is helpful. He argued that capitalist apologists attribute their success to the benign operations of individual market transactions when it really should be attributed to the malignant exercise of social power. Marx had considerable if grudging respect for capitalism, acknowledging its enormous material successes, but insisting that brutality was not a mere side effect. Capitalism entailed the separation of the majority of producers from the means of production—especially land—what he called primitive accumulation. He attributed the emergence of England as the world's great economic power to the violent extinction of the rights of its people to access to land. Expropriation not only left the majority with no choice but to sell the one asset they had—their labor power—but it left land and factory owners with no choice but to buy it. Capitalism was more successful in the long run than household production, serfdom, or slavery—and one could now add communism—because it compelled property owners to compete each day to hire labor and therefore to employ that labor power as efficiently as everyone else. The slaveowner in need of more income could be more brutal; the peasant could survive from household production if crop markets turned against him. Capitalist and wage-worker were bound together—unequally—in the labor market.[21]

Relation

The actual forms of labor that characterized nineteenth-century Europe—let alone the colonies—did not conform to the pure notion of wage labor posited in Marxist theory. A wide range of forms of coercion were important to the recruitment of labor and to the labor process itself, within factories or on fields.[22] But the ambiguous basis of wage labor made it all the more important for elites to represent it as a distinct form of work. And it would be hard to do so if the slave stolen from Africa and laboring under the whip on a Jamaican sugar plantation could not be sharply distinguished from the English worker in a textile mill, who had been driven into the factory by deprivation—by the extinction of forms of tenancy that had given at least some access to land, by the destruction of artisanal privileges, and by the erosion of a more paternalistic model of class relations.

In this sense, the effort of humanitarian activists in the late eighteenth and early nineteenth to define the slave trade and slavery as evils helped, whatever those activists' intentions, to define the specificity and acceptability of wage labor. Antislavery activism was not a bourgeois conspiracy, and there were working class activists who sought to tar with the label "wage slavery" the forms of labor subordination characteristic of English factories, but those activists were not the ones who succeeded in framing the slavery question. The act of Parliament of 1833 that finally abolished slavery in the British West Indies represented a conservative version of antislavery—requiring freed slaves to go through a period of "apprenticeship" even though they knew perfectly well how to cut cane—and it was nearly simultaneous with Poor Law legislation in England that made life harsher for the working class in Britain.[23]

This brings us to the point where Marx's Eurocentric point of view led him astray. In his writing on India, Marx predicted that the brutality of British conquest would have effects similar to that of the brutality of primitive accumulation in England: to force Indian upper classes to give up their backward Hindu ways and to exploit their subalterns in proper capitalist fashion.[24] Yet the impact of British power in India was not to undo Indian social structure, but in a selective way to reinforce it. Indian landlords were the key to revenue collection by the state.[25] British writers at the time did not discuss this process in terms of the limits of colonial power or as evidence that distinct paths to the future might emerge; they told a tale of Indian backwardness, much as Africa's twentieth-century economy would be represented as Africans' primitive nature.

From the 1850s, European travelers to Africa used images of backwardness and violence to describe a continent crying out for European intervention. The slave trade, which European money had done so much to stimulate, became a central image of Africa. David Livingstone's voyages gave publicity to a view of the African—once the Enslaved Victim—as the Enslaving Tyrant.[26] Colonization was now advocated as the only way to save Africans from their own violence and tyranny and to "open"—a favorite metaphor—the continent to the beneficial effects of legitimate commerce. The motives behind colonization were of course more complex and hardly benign. Nevertheless, images of oppression and backwardness were extended from areas where the slave trade was supplying African slaveowners to parts of Africa where slavery was not significant at all. Colonization could be normalized because the colonized could be represented as outside the boundaries of normality.

Orientalism

The impetus behind reformist imperialism barely lasted a couple of decades. Colonial rulers soon found that they could maintain order only by forging alliances with the very elites whose tyranny and economic irrationality they had railed against, and colonialism in most of the continent soon settled for living off the surplus production of peasants, the coercive extraction of valuable raw materials, or the employment of laborers who retained a strong foothold in their villages, lowering their cost but also assuring that they gave only part of their being to the demands of production and export.[27]

European colonizers were profiting from and exacerbating an intersection of possibilities and constraints similar to those that underlay the slave trade—African societies' "extroversion," to use Jean-François Bayart's phrase, their relative resistance to internal exploitation and adaptability to external economic relations.[28] The mediocrity of colonial economies was not a major problem for their rulers when the costs of overseas government were low. World-spanning empires could focus on a few areas with valuable resources, including only those parts of Africa that constituted what a French banker in the 1930s called "useful Africa."[29] The most exploitative of colonial interventions—the actions of concessionary companies to extract resources like rubber or the forced cultivation of cotton in Portuguese Mozambique, Belgian Congo, or French Equatorial Africa—were notable for their brutality, not their capacity for systematic, long-term development of human and natural resources.[30]

The weakness of colonial power made it more violent, not less, but not so certain in its effects. Africans in much of the continent had considerable social resources, and they used mobility, kinship networks, and the ability to move between modes of economic activity to avoid too much dependence on white employers in mines or cities or would-be African capitalists in the countryside. It was mainly in South Africa that a racialized version of Marx's primitive accumulation took shape.

Such a process emerged from South Africa's particular trajectory. Going back to 1652, a white settler population of Dutch and later British origin established itself on the land, extracting rents, labor, and crop shares from African inhabitants, leaving most peasants to keep actual production in their own hands. The discovery of diamonds in 1866 and gold in 1886 escalated the demand for a large labor force. With improved infrastructure, a growing non-farming population, and a government willing to use bureaucracy and coercion to channel workers into wage labor, white farmers had new incentives to tighten control over their land, expel tenants, and employ wage labor in agriculture.[31] Mineowners and the government could make use of a distinct category of people, whites, to supervise African workers on the job, enforce land alienation, and put into play a series of laws—segregated spaces, pass laws that punished Africans in "white" areas when not actually at work, and reinforcement of chieftaincies—to keep a black labor force in its place. Africans sought to find niches in the system, but over time, the combination of power in the hands of government and employers reduced those alternatives.[32]

Elsewhere in Africa there were enclaves of wage labor—the copper mines of the Belgian Congo and the British Rhodesias, the settler farms of Kenya or Côte d'Ivoire—but they drew on migrant labor whose access to land was constrained but not eliminated as it largely was in South Africa. A readily exploitable mining or plantation zone required a much larger labor catchment area around it where alternative sources of cash income were, deliberately or otherwise, limited.

In most of Africa, colonial governments invested little, until after World War II, when they had to confront the consequences of colonial stagnation.[33] The railway map of Africa (next page)—emerging in a time when railroads were both the sign and substance of economic relations—is highly revealing: a small number of railway lines, mostly narrow-gauge, draining limited hinterlands toward port cities, and, outside of South Africa, virtually no lines connecting parts of Africa with each other—this in contrast to India as much as to western and eastern Europe.

British and French rulers began in the 1920s to pretend that their inability to remake Africa was really the success of a policy of conserving African culture and slowly changing it within Africans' allegedly limited capabilities. Their conservative policies were compatible with expanded crop production, as Africans' kinship and personal ties proved capable of responding to market incentives and mobilizing resources.

The most notable African success stories in this regard—cocoa in Gold Coast, Nigeria, and the Côte d'Ivoire—were based on flexible relations of production that cannot be reduced to either "peasant" or "capitalist." The first cocoa bushes came from Swiss missionaries to the Gold Coast in the late nineteenth century, when British power was essentially limited to a few coastal locations. A small number of Africans, living inland from the coast, with little encouragement from British officials, began to cultivate the crop and sell the cocoa that came from pods on the bush. The groups

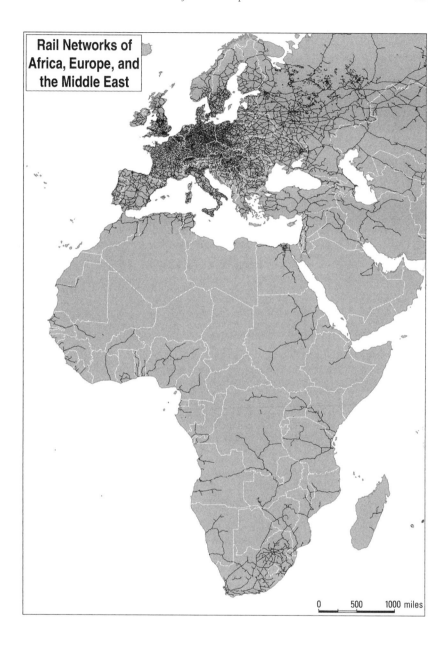

Rail Networks of
Africa, Europe, and
the Middle East

0   500   1000 miles

that controlled good cocoa land leased or granted it to entrepreneurial strangers, who in turn mobilized kinfolk and others to help them plant trees and subsist until the trees were bearing. Much labor came from migrants or people who formed long-term relations of clientage as from formal wage labor relations. Laborers sought the patronage of the cocoa planter and had some expectations that inserting themselves into the production process might, over time and with the successful manipulation of personal relations, allow them to become planters too.

What is remarkable about the cocoa boom of the turn of the twentieth century was that it takes several years for a cocoa bush to reach production, so that the entrepreneurs who took up this crop were both thinking ahead and mobilizing resources—labor, food—in anticipation of deriving an income from the commodity. The story also points to the importance of looking beyond one form—supposedly "western"—of land tenure as the key to innovation and growth. Cocoa production advanced in the absence of freehold ownership, through sharing of rights in productive resources among those with original rights to land, those who added the most productive new resource—cocoa bushes—and kinsmen and clients whose long-term labor might give them access to resources too. This system of land tenure reached a limit of exploitation. Planters could not expand too far, exploit workers too intensely, or constrain others from gaining access to resources because their security of tenure and access to labor depended on connections of community and clientage. Sara Berry describes the outcome as "exploitation without appropriation."[34]

Colonial regimes never quite recognized the significance of this form of economic innovation, even if they enjoyed the export revenue: Africans were not only producing valuable crops, but they were doing so in their own flexible ways. In cocoa-producing regions, some family members could farm, others work for wages, others seek education. But could the very inventiveness and flexibility of these social systems—the obstacles they posed to tyranny and exploitation—have made it more difficult for either Africans or their invaders to perfect patterns of systematic exploitation that underlay capitalist development? Cocoa production seemed to follow a cyclical pattern, constrained both by the need for new resources to maintain the possibility of upward mobility and by the political-economic context in which cocoa production took place. By the 1930s in the Gold Coast, less land was available for new entrants to the cocoa business and a cocoa-growing elite had differentiated itself from the rest of the population, giving rise to social tensions between the large-scale cocoa farmers and the small-scale farmers and agricultural workers.[35] In the 1950s and 1960s, cocoa farmers came into conflict with an African-controlled government now eager to control resources itself. The cocoa farmers reacted by curtailing the renewal of the cocoa bushes, and by the mid-1960s cocoa production in independent Ghana was plummeting. Some years behind the Gold Coast farmers, a similar cycle of extensive expansion followed some decades later by contraction began in western Nigeria, lasting until the 1980s. In this case, growing oil revenues gave rise to so much employment, in the state sector and otherwise, that laborers for a time found more attractive alternatives to the cocoa economy, while the sons of affluent planters found more lucrative opportunities in the state or other businesses.[36] In the Côte d'Ivoire after 1946, the end of forced labor directed toward European farmers gave African farmers a chance to organize labor and production in their own ways, giving rise to what has been called the "Ivorian miracle" that lasted until the bottom fell out of the cocoa market in the 1990s. What distinguished all of these upward cycles was that they involved a relatively large population and promoted linkages to other economic activities. One cannot say the same about the exportation of oil (which demands few workers) or plantation economies dominated by small—often foreign—landowning elites, using cheap and insecure wage labor.[37]

In the late 1940s and early 1950s, when the Gold Coast, Nigeria, and Côte d'Ivoire were generating considerable wealth through agricultural exports, officials—including specialists in colonial economies—in London and Paris were not always able to recognize that they were onto a good thing, although local officials were more wont to boast of their success. The experts in colonial economy were too steeped in images of African backwardness, too wedded to European-centered models of what systems of production should look like, to understand the alternative pathways forward, let alone their limitations. To take examples from French West Africa, a conference on reviewing plans for development projects was told that "Unfortunately, this agriculture is entirely in the hands of Africans, and for this reason its development will certainly be fairly slow, because it will be necessary to act on the native, to teach him to rationalize his methods, to improve his product. . . ." A governor insisted that one had to press development projects in the face of a population that remained "frozen in anachronistic and archaic concepts and does not see the necessity to participate by a voluntary and reasoned effort in the progress of their country. *On the whole the masses are not yet socially ready to adapt to the norms of a renovated life.*"[38] Similarly in Great Britain, the Minister in charge of the Colonial Office and some of his economics staff were specifically calling for an "agricultural revolution" in Africa, without understanding the dynamics of production that were actually taking place.[39]

The interventionist impetus behind these remarks reflected new thinking on the part of British and French governments in the 1940s, including realization that their own contribution to economic growth had been inadequate: minimal construction of railroads, roads, and port facilities, lack of investment in processing of African raw materials or in local manufacturing, miserable living conditions in cities, and meager health and educational facilities. They finally enacted programs—rejected by both governments in the 1920s and 1930s—to use metropolitan funds to improve the infrastructure and social services they deemed necessary to promote economic development.[40] The embrace of the development concept was in part a reaction to disorders that had struck the British (and to a more limited extent French) empires during the late 1930s, during the war, and in the years following World War II. These disorders were concentrated not in the poorest parts of the empires, but in areas where commercial activity and wage workers—and much human misery—were concentrated, in mines, railroads, commercial centers, and ports. "Development" was supposed to make the empires more productive—and thereby aid France and Britain to recover from the war—but also more legitimate.

But development initiatives in the 1950s were circumscribed not only by the economic weaknesses of European powers that they were supposed to overcome—inadequate state finances in particular—and by the poor quality of the colonial infrastructure on which to build, but by a failure of imagination. When colonial regimes after World War II returned to their older transformative zeal, seeking to make Africa more productive and to legitimize their rule by raising its standard of living, they were caught in their brittle dualism of "modern" and "backward" economies. As they began to act as if Africans could be made into regular wage laborers, good farmers, and urban property owners, they contrasted their imagined acultural, asocial, modern African to the backward tribalist—missing the change and innovation that had occurred outside of this imagined polarity.[41]

By now, African workers in ports, mines, and railways were in a position to insist—in a wave of post-war strikes—that they share in economic growth. The very narrowness of colonial transformations in the previous half-century meant that disruption in key transportation nodes or in mines by relatively small numbers of people tied together in networks that colonial police did not understand had a relatively large impact. The sudden increase in investment clogged the narrow channels that regimes controlled.[42] The development effort—intended in part to convince angry workers and peasants that European-directed modernization would improve their standard of living—led instead to more conflict.

African labor movements were actively engaging with the new colonial politics of development. If we are to produce like European workers, they insisted, we should receive equal pay for equal work. Africans coopted into legislative institutions in France turned the argument that French political institutions and culture were the model for Africa into a claim to the entitlements of French citizens.

That was only one side of the politics of the post-war decade; mobilization also took place through a variety of cultural mechanisms, through peasant movements, local healers, kinship group elders, and organizations of women.[43] The protests of the late 1940s and 1950s were effective because of the conjuncture of different forms of political action. Social and political movements did more than force changes in government. In the 1950s they decisively changed international discourse about colonialism, national self-determination, economic development, and Africa.

The people who should have been the success stories of economic growth in this era—the cocoa producers of Western Nigeria or the coffee growers of northern Tanganyika—used their earnings to enhance their importance in their communities, to forge networks of clients and supporters, to invest in marketing independent of the colonial firms, and to fund political parties that supported their interests against the colonial state. Where such routes were blocked, as in Central Kenya or Algeria, violent struggles ensued, and colonial regimes reacted in a way that revealed the brittleness of their own conceptions of Africa. Africans who would not accept the version of modernization on offer were labeled atavistic and dangerous and subjected to fierce repression at the same time that regimes were calmly negotiating with African leaders in the Gold

Coast or French West Africa.[44] In the end, colonial governments realized that the predicable, orderly, and productive Africa that development was supposed to produce was not springing into existence and that their reformism was providing new languages in which aggressive social and political movements could assert themselves. France and Britain began to reassess the costs and benefits of the African colonies as they actually were. The cold calculations have left their traces in the archives: by mid-1950s the accountants in France and Great Britain reported that African colonies did not necessarily pay.[45]

South Africa, from the mid-1940s to the late 1980s, seemed to be moving in a contrary direction. Beset by some of the same forces as French and British Africa, including workers demanding higher wages during World War II and some major employers seeking to create a stable urban working class that would serve its interests, the South African government decided otherwise after the 1948 election. It chose to deepen segregation and maintain a dependent labor force on farms and migrant workers in the gold mines. It escalated repression rather than seek to coopt an African elite. The result was "apartheid." South Africa would sustain racial domination as a *national* project even when it was being formally abandoned as an *imperial* project by the two leading European powers. Racialized capitalism sustained South African industrialization. The edifice began to crack only when South African whites, who felt themselves to be the embodiments of Christian civilization and bourgeois entitlement, began to feel the pinch of global pariah status. Major enterprises ran into difficulties in attracting capital and sought alternative arrangements. The escalation of violence during the 1980s—some of it the result of activists' campaigns to make South Africa "ungovernable," some of it resulting from the tensions within vulnerable and deprived African communities—led South African elites to the realization that racial domination in one country was not sustainable.

In most of Africa what followed colonial rule, some would say, was not independence in any but the most technical sense, but neo-colonialism. The trouble with this reasoning is that it is a simple answer where a good question is in order: what are the ways in which power is exercised over formally sovereign states? What African elites won was sovereignty and little but sovereignty—and that became a card they had to play at home and abroad. Sovereignty meant that the once-colonial concept of development became a national concept—one that could be used for a ruling elite's ends or else by people who saw meager results from government policies to challenge African rulers.

In international circles, the idea of development policy has been attacked from the right—as an impediment to the optimizing operations of free markets—and from the left as an imposition of an unwanted modernity and a project to make Africa safe for global capitalism. But one should be careful about generalizations about a varied process that bridges the moment of independence, from the late 1940s to at least the 1970s. These decades were a time when in a wide range of African countries average life span increased, infant mortality declined, literacy expanded, higher education took off from virtually nothing to something significant. And despite population growth, GNP per capita edged modestly upward in much of Africa. The decline in such figures—particularly social indicators—came later, especially in the 1980s.

Africa was particularly hard hit and particularly slow to recover from the world recession of the mid-1970s that followed a spike in oil prices and a crisis in availability of credit as well as a changed monetary system that produced instability. World recession meant decreased demand for African primary materials, and African states were still dependent on imported manufactured goods and—all the more so because of their efforts at development—on imported petroleum products whose prices were skyrocketing. As government revenue fell, states became more dependent on international financial institutions to pay their debts and meet their most basic import needs. And those institutions were in the thrall of a god that commanded "structural adjustment." In the name of market openness and financial rigor, African states were ordered to cut their budgets, lay off personnel, curtail protection of infant industries, and end the subsidies that enabled many workers to buy consumer goods. If that meant devastating cuts in education and other social services, so be it. In some quarters, structural adjustment was an explicit disavowal of the development project that had animated economic policy since the 1940s.[46]

Arguments about development go round and round, but let me try to put the issue in a long-term historical context. The development concept at one level represented poverty as the eternal backwardness of Africa to be ameliorated by the benevolent injection of western knowledge, markets, and capital. At another level, discussion of poverty eradication made development into a framework for the posing of demands by social and political movements in Africa—and eventually some African governments—for a kind of global social citizenship. Rulers have been criticized for failure to bring about development, even as they used the idea of a "battle for development" to justify their own authoritarian excesses. The very global hierarchy conveyed in this construct implies that the poverty of Mali is an issue in Denmark, just as antislavery ideology made labor conditions in Jamaica or Zanzibar a concern in London, while colonialism and apartheid could be issues in New York or Cambridge.[47]

The central point is that the problem is not one of Africa's aboriginal poverty, but of structures that are Afro-European creations.[48] Some of these are the institutions that have proved adaptive—too adaptive—to changing historical circumstances. Some leaders and their followers responded effectively to the growing market for slaves in the sixteenth century or for slave-produced commodities in the nineteenth century. Others used mobility and kinship ties to escape such predations. Similarly, some Africans used social networks and geographic flexibility to avoid too much dependence on wage labor or too complete subordination to white-dominated states in the colonial era, while others made use of the relatively narrow channels of export economies to obtain a moderate degree of wealth for themselves and their immediate communities.

What this history has produced are "gatekeeper states."[49] Gatekeeper states, like colonial states, are strong at the nodal point where local society meets external economy, dependent on manipulating revenues and patronage possibilities deriving from that point, including foreign aid and commercial deals. They are also vulnerable to challenges to control of the node. Not only were they subject to coups or attempts to gain control of resources independent of the state, but they also feared a politics of citizenship that might challenge the vertical mechanisms of control—from patrons to clients to regional or ethnic power brokers—that gatekeeping fostered. Such fears were realistic. Gatekeeping elites risked being challenged by armed networks seeking a way around the gate: the civil war in Angola in the 1990s, with the state controlling oil revenues and the rebels controlling diamonds, is a classic case. Violent conflict in turn was a blow to economic and social development and an inducement to enroll young men in predatory networks of clientage.[50]

Gatekeeping would not be a viable strategy but for the extreme asymmetry in economic relations between Africa and the industrial countries. Certain individuals and groups, on both sides, have a vested interest in keeping things as they are—to make their deals, to monopolize key resources, to profit from the private provision of services that are in most countries public. When the international financial organizations in the 1980s argued that they could reduce "rent seeking" by governmental elites by shrinking the state, gatekeeping elites were likely to shrink public services—notably education and public health—rather than their rents, and privatization did not necessarily imply competition.[51]

The clearest exception to gatekeeping strategies by African rulers is South Africa, where the effects of the long process of creating racialized capitalism has left in place industry, wage-labor agriculture, and a working class. The big question is whether there is enough work for the working class. Unemployment is crushingly high. The affluent elite—and a good portion of the middle class—are no longer exclusively white, and the fact that one can be rich without being in power is an element in political stability. South Africa has changed dramatically since the end of apartheid, but it remains one of the most unequal societies in the world.[52]

Looking back, the very experience of mobilization against colonialism in the late 1940s and 1950s—in which labor unions, farmers' organizations, and student associations had made claims to a place in the political arena and a share in resources—made elites wary that such ideas could be turned against them, and they were conscious of how limited their resources were to meet such demands. Development was too important as a source of manipulable patronage resources and as a symbol of the state's gatekeeper power to be allowed to take a course toward private accumulation or toward letting trade unions, farmers' associations, and other organizations independent of the state take the initiative. Colonial governments had learned to live with the limitations of their power to remake Africa. Their more interventionist efforts at the beginning and at the end of their period of rule fell short, and the new African governments had fewer means than their imperial predecessors.

What can this rapid excursion through African economic history since the fifteenth century tell us about Africa's present situation? One of the most influential attempts to answer such a question comes from Daron Acemoglu and James Robinson, whose work has the virtue of turning the culturalist explanation for Africa's lag in economic development into an institutionalist one. Africa suffers from bad institutions, they argue, and those institutions are a consequence of the history of the slave trade and

colonialism, not just African culture or institutions rooted in Africa's earlier past.[53] But there are problems with this approach. One is that the
institutional argument presumes that Europe is in the only model for economic growth, so one should take European institutions—such as private
property in land—and then treat any deviation from them as the explanation for why another place lags behind. But what if there is more than one
route forward, as Asianists have been arguing? A second problem is that
the institutional argument hinges on showing that the differential impact
across the African continent of, say, the slave trade can be shown to correlate with unevenness in patterns of economic growth in the present,
without looking at historical processes in sequence.[54] Finally there is the
question of defining what one is trying to explain. Here, the economic
historian Morten Jerven has made an insightful intervention: generaliz-
ing about lack of growth is not the issue. Jerven points out that different
parts of Africa have had a series of spurts, in which economic growth has
been strong by world standards. He cites parts of West Africa in the era
of the slave trade, the cocoa boom in West Africa in the colonial era, and
the export boom of the 1950s and 1960s, plus—more ambiguously—
the recent revival of exports. The 1980s, however, were a time of severe
contraction.[55]

This observation gives us a different focus—on unevenness, in spatial,
social, and political terms. What can historical analysis tell us about particular forms of asymmetrical connections and their consequences? The
transactions between the seller of slaves and the final buyer linked people
who had their own interests, networks, and conceptions. It was also at the
point of connection that colonial regimes exercised most authority, unable
as they most often were to effectively control—let alone economically
transform—the countryside. Making connections was not just a matter of
coercion, but of the creation of incentives for elites in specific areas to
deploy the human resources they had to get what they could. A world-
spanning empire—or for that matter transnational corporations—could
write off regions of less interest or leave them to supply low-cost labor. It
was not, for example, only the paucity of French investment in infrastructure in colonial West Africa but its uneven distribution that is echoed in
highly unequal distribution of economic resources today.[56] Such structures were quite effective—at low cost to the state—at adapting to certain
world market incentives, but vulnerable both to market fluctuations and
to challenges of other social formations or other sources of patronage.

Africa has proved both adaptable to some forms of interaction and resilient in the face of others. Africans live with the consequences of both their adaptation to external markets, foreign conquest, and the narrow channels of colonial and post-colonial economies and with the ability of many of them to maintain access to land and to avoid total submergence in a wage labor system. Would many of them be better off—as the working classes of Europe eventually were—if the triumph of capitalism in Africa had been more complete, if their subjection to overseas settlers and extractive industries was more thorough, if the grandiose projects of colonial and independent regimes had been more successful—at whatever human cost? Perhaps—or perhaps not. In any case, the multiple sites of European empire and later the mobility of transnational corporations meant that imperial powers did not have to succeed in subjugating all the world—they could be selective. And the complex adaptations of forms of production and exchange that Africans have in fact made have not produced universal immiseration but a more mixed and shifting record.

One of Jerven's main growth spurts, from the 1950s to the early 1970s, occurred at a time when many governments, colonial and national, were spending more than before or since on education, health, and—for wage workers at least—the rudiments of a welfare state, including wages intended to support a family, pensions, housing, and medical care. In the subsequent period, when African countries were forced to dismantle such social spending and follow market-oriented policies, the growth record was worse.[57]

One cannot say that African leaders generally succeeded in meeting their frequently stated goal after independence of economic autonomy. Some of them, however, did quite well by other criteria—enriching themselves and staying in power. Omar Bongo, who ruled Gabon for 40 years and passed the presidency to his son or Félix Houphouët-Boigny, who ruled Côte d'Ivoire for 33 years, are cases in point. The gatekeeper state could be modestly development-oriented in policy and consequences, but the measures intended to shrink it had the perverse effect of undermining the development without ending the gatekeeping. Here lies the crux of the matter: the vast divergence in the world economy means leaders are behaving quite rationally in thinking it better to control a small pie than to follow "experts'" recipies for how, in the long-run, to make the pie bigger. Gatekeeping has fostered both self-aggrandizing rulers and violent conflict over the gate, with even more dire results.

For people at the bottom—or even the middle—of the hierarchy, seeking a patron is often a more hopeful strategy than organizing collectively among the poor or playing by the rules of a "formal" economy. And African entrepreneurs have a long history of developing linkages and adapting methods of economic interaction to the situation at hand.

The past ten years are considered by some observers to be a period of progress, when some African countries have experienced growth rates higher than the world average. For the first time since the 1970s, overall poverty rates for the region have declined.[58] Once again, the record is mixed. Jerven's growth-spurt model is probably what fits best. The expansion is heavily based on extractive industry, fueled by the sharp increase in demand for raw materials from China and India. Mines—and especially oil platforms—"work in enclaves that are more or less cut off from the societies in which they exist."[59] That Angolan exports, largely oil, have shot upward does not mean that most Angolans have benefitted. Botswana and Ghana offer more hope, with considerable uncertainty over how profound and durable the changes are. Telecommunications has been another growth area, and the advent of the cell phone has made a real difference for African consumers, even more so for those favored investors who could get government franchises. The cell phone not only frees users from the limited, unreliable, and expensive network of land lines, but provides a divisible resource, something people of modest income can pay for bit by bit. In cities like Dakar, there are armies of young men in the streets selling phone cards, evidence of adaptability to a market niche, but also a sign of the desperation of such people for the meager income street selling will get them.

Some areas of Africa—northern Mali, Somalia, and the region along the new Sudan-Southern Sudan border—are mired in conflict that undermines the well-being of large numbers of people. Others, like Sierra Leone, are slowly recovering. Whether we are likely to see radical, sustained, or generalized transformation out of this growth spurt remains unclear.[60]

If we wish to look forward, we can make a few simple points. The economic problems and vulnerabilities of Africa are not intrinsic characteristics of the continent, but consequences of a Euro-African history, of patterns established by both positive responses to the possibilities of interaction and by resistance to submergence in colonial economies. It is doubtful that solutions can be found without questioning global structures of economic power as well as Africa's supposed deviations from preset norms.

The idea that the current resources of all African countries—Mali and Chad as well as the Congo or Nigeria—are adequate to provide the infrastructure for twenty-first century economic development is implausible. Some dimensions of development are best handled on a small scale, others not. One study suggests that in average districts of former French West Africa 14 percent of households have electricity, 11 percent private water supply, 15 percent gas or electricity for cooking, and variation among districts is very large, so that many parts of the region are considerably worse off than the averages suggest.[61] One does not improve infrastructure like this without large investment, and one does not produce a skilled labor force or attract industry in such conditions. Building a country-wide health service or quality secondary education for an entire population is not likely to happen unaided in impoverished countries and is not likely to be sustained when export-led booms come to an end. For all the now-familiar problems of foreign aid, we should ask what use it is to consider it "foreign" when the histories of Africa and of the rest of the world have been intertwined for so long.

The one-size-fits-all solutions for Africa's problems that have come from outside and inside do not have a strong track record.[62] The "magic of the market" touted in the 1980s proved not very magical. So-called African socialism and experiments with economic nationalism—import substitution industrialization, state corporations, collective farms or forced villagization—have gone badly too. But perhaps the peasant cocoa farmers of southern Ghana or the market women of West Africa have lessons to teach us. Recently, experiments in Niger of intercropping trees and food crops have produced more positive results than decades of imposed policies of defining forest reserves and clearing bush for farms elsewhere.[63]

African forms of land tenure—which have produced both flexibility and tensions—have shown themselves quite capable of fostering agricultural development. If one followed the logic of taking institutions that have seemed conducive to economic growth in Europe as models for what Africans should do, one might be tempted to say that Africans need to make land into an alienable commodity and create an open market in land, including the possibility of selling land, in whatever size chunks, to foreigners. In fact, several African countries—including Ethiopia, Mozambique, and Sudan—have alienated enormous parcels of land to Brazilian, Indian, and Korean enterprises, without clear indication of what the impact of such sales will be on Africans' future farming possibilities,

Promoted solution

on the availability and cost of food, and on labor conditions. Knowledgeable observers fear, with good reason, that deeper impoverishment is a more likely outcome of such processes than economic takeoff. Some countries that have alienated huge plots for the export of food crops are themselves recipients of food aid.[64]

A great deal is left unexamined if Africa is understood as everything Europe pretended not to be. Can we see the openings—admitting their limitations—that particular systems of production or specific marketing networks provide, without falling into the false dichotomy of free market and closed state? Perhaps in positing "Africa" as the problem, we are looking both too broadly and too narrowly: too narrowly to see the long history that linked the peoples inhabiting the African continent to the expansion of capitalism, too broadly to see the different ways in which production and commerce across that space have actually worked.

To think of a backward Africa against a modern world or a benign Africa against a hostile world does not get us far. No part of the world has had or can hope to have a self-contained existence, any more than markets function outside of the relationships out of which they were constructed. Africa and Europe shaped each other, but not through symmetrical processes. The world today does not consist of equivalent nation-states any more than the "world market" consists of equivalent actors. To see an Africa, Asia, or Europe whose economic "performance" can be compared with each other obscures both the historical mechanisms through which such entities were imagined and constituted and the nature of international connections today. Unequal struggle is the reality faced today as well as in the past.

Africans, individually and collectively, through networks, kingdoms, local communities, and nation-states, have adapted well—sometimes frighteningly well—to the possibilities that external linkages presented, but they have also made it difficult for kings, colonizers, and capitalists to subordinate them. Adaptation and resistance have had their consequences not only in Africa's economic vulnerability, but in the way it is talked about. One might nonetheless ask not only about how African polities can conform to the institutional structure set up by others, but how international financial institutions or European and American policies of subsidizing agriculture and setting tariffs, credit mechanisms, and rules governing commerce and investment can be altered to benefit the poorest of poor states. One might ask how countries with few material and organizational resources within their borders can be helped to make the necessary investments in education and health and develop the institutional capacity to regulate labor conditions and commercial transactions without which social progress and economic advance will not be achieved in the future. The problem with thinking of Africa as peculiar and other places as normal is that such questions do not get asked.

2

∽o∽

Africa and Empire

The idea of empire was configured in two ways in Du Bois's *The World and Africa*. He argued that Africans were perfectly capable of putting together large-scale, coherently organized polities. He wrote about the early African empires, from the Nile Valley to the great empires of Ghana, Mali, and Songhay, and described the expansion of Asante into a vast state capable of ruling over diverse populations. He also examined the colonization of Africa by Europeans.

Du Bois had read the best historical scholarship of his time on the early history of Africa—limited as it was—and he knew perfectly well that empires in Africa did what empires usually do. They engaged in violent conquest, extended their rule over people who regarded themselves as distinct, extracted tribute and resources from the people they subjugated, and—in some situations—sold the captives of military operations. But that was not Du Bois's focus. Instead, he wanted to demonstrate Africans' political capabilities across history.

European empires appeared in a different light in his work. After pointing to the imminent collapse of European domination as a result of World War II, he turned to a discussion of racism and then of the slave trade. Here lay the responsibility for crushing the progress of which African polities were capable and—of equal importance—for inscribing backwardness on the dynamic history of Africa. Whatever the sins of African empires, associating a race with inferiority or backwardness was not one of them. The indictment of racialized empire resonated with one of Du Bois's most famous lines, dating to 1903, "The problem of the twentieth century is the problem of the color line."[1]

The word in this pronouncement that has perhaps received the least attention is "problem." Du Bois was doing his best, in 1946 as in 1903, to make sure that the color line would be a problem. He was combating one of the most insidious aspects of race thinking: the naturalization of racial distinctions and racial hierarchies, the sense that this was the way the world operates. He was not alone in doing so; there never was a period in which white domination was uncontested, even during the period of reaction in the United States and colonial conquest in Africa at the turn of the century. Still, when Du Bois wrote about the problem of the color bar, he had a tough task before him. But at the time of Du Bois's *The World and Africa,* nearly a half-century and two world wars later, the efforts of colonial ideologues to justify white rule over black people were unraveling.

So too was empire, or at least it was beginning to do so. Empire, in one form or another, has a very long history, alongside which the concepts of nation-state, popular sovereignty, and self-determination have a short and possibly transient existence. Africans had forged empires from the time of Aksum to that of Haile Selassie of Ethiopia. The latter—a self-styled emperor whose rule was personal and autocratic—could be proclaimed a hero by those who opposed European empire for his courageous but vain struggle to resist an empire-builder of the 1930s, Benito Mussolini. Haile Selassie's empire would outlast those of the Italians, French, and British, but it too would be caught up in the changes in the world political order and come crashing down in 1974.

Here we focus on the empire in both of Du Bois's senses—as a general political form that Africa shared with the rest of the world and as a specific form, the colonial empires constructed by Europe in Africa in the nineteenth and twentieth centuries.[2] Putting the two together by no means diminishes the force of the indictment of colonialism. Instead, it turns the focus from the name of empire to the substance of different imperial regimes. And it takes the discussion out of a presumed narrative that leads inexorably from empire to nation-state, a pathway held to be both historically correct and normative. Instead, it asks where people, at different points in the story, actually wanted to go. In looking at the past, by freeing ourselves from the presumed normality of the nation-state form—one people, one territory, one government—we can better understand both the importance and the limitations of the political units that actually were imagined and constructed at different points of history. We can contextualize as well the self-representations of European empire-builders as the model for progress.

Empires are large, expansionist political units that preserve and reproduce differences among the peoples and places they incorporate. In other words, empires govern different people differently. If the ruling fiction of the nation-state is homogeneity, the ruling fiction of empire is the management and exploitation of difference, and the practice of empires comes closer than that of nation-states to embodying its fiction, unbothered as empires are by the need to pretend they are treating subjects alike.

Empires' politics of difference took different forms. The Mongol model treated the distinctiveness of conquered people in a matter-of-fact way, something to be either exploited as a strategy of rule or ignored, leaving subdued peoples to go their own way as long as they paid tribute and caused no trouble. The Roman model posited a singular, superior civilization to which others—particularly the elites of conquered regions—might aspire. Empires could entrench invidious distinctions—in cultural and racial terms. At an extreme, they might turn the diverse populations they incorporated into something like a homogenizing nation-state via assimilation, extermination, or a combination of the two. That empires confronted difference explicitly does not mean that they did so in a benign way.

Empires had shifting repertoires of rule, often employing different strategies in different places at the same time. The ability to shift the balance among different elements of an imperial repertoire contributed to the longevity of some empires—for example, the Ottoman's six-hundred-year history or the more than two thousand years in which Chinese dynasties claimed the mantle of their predecessors. It is too early to tell if the nation-state will have such a long life span.

Europeans' images of Africa in the time of colonial rule relied so much on the notion of tribe that they were hard put to see beyond it. But when one penetrates the notion of indigeneity—the idea of Africans living for

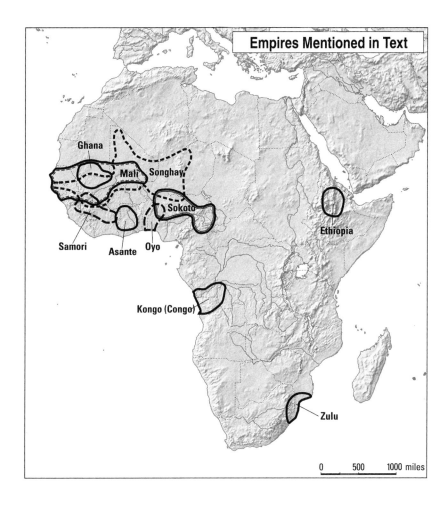

Empires Mentioned in Text

centuries, if not since the dawn of time, in solidarity with their kinsmen and preserving a singular, stable culture—it fails to account for the history of the continent. African historians for some time have emphasized that ethnic affinity has been both important and volatile. Many peoples have been highly mobile, and even those who were attached to localities were in contact with those who were in motion. Large political entities both incorporated diverse communities and spun off others.

The concept of empire is useful in African history, not just to remake Du Bois's point that Africans could create empires too, but to explore the variations on the empire form that one finds around the world, particularly the different ways in which the extension of political power over diverse populations played out historically.

In the savanna regions of West Africa, populations concentrated at a few particularly desirable points such as along the Niger River or at junctures of trade routes connecting the savanna regions with either the desert or the forest zone to the south. The rest of the area supported relatively spread-out populations, some of them highly mobile, engaged in trade pastoralism, others more sedentary, mixing agriculture and pastoralism. In such a situation, it was relatively feasible for a group of people with some advantage—a relatively large population, good connections to long-distance trading networks, control of a valuable resource like salt, iron, or gold, or the skill or charisma of a leader—to attract followers. An expanding collectivity appealed above all to people whose own social ties had loosened. With more human and material resources, the leaders of such a community could marry more women and expand their lineage and they could incorporate captives into the society, thus creating a disequilibrium among the social groups of the region.

If such an entity could over a few generations consolidate its power and develop authoritative military, administrative, and judicial institutions, it could continue over a long period of time to incorporate people and to create an incentive for more and more local elders or chiefs to cooperate. The art of governing was above all that of balancing the attractiveness, authority, and coercive capacity of the growing center with recognition of the distinct cultural and political affinities of incorporated people. African empires, like many others, grew up knowing about other empires and seeing themselves in relation to them.

As Susan Keech McIntosh points out, African data fit rather uneasily into conventional models of building large-scale polities, such as the notion that centralization should go along with growing population density. "A variety of African societies move back and forth from lineage to village headship to regional chiefship and kingship." Africa witnessed "diverse pathways" to complex political structures.[3] Such fluidity was compatible with empire-building on a large spacial scale. The empire form was adaptable to such situations as rulers could provide integration into larger, wealth-gathering structures without undermining kinship or village-level structures. These patterns could lead to important social dynamics— the spread of Islam in Sahelian West Africa for instance—that survived even when the political form changed. But because the resources that provided advantage to an empire-centered network depended on external linkages, the structures could also be volatile, as in the conflict-ridden politics of West-Central Africa (present-day Congo and Angola), linked to Portuguese and Dutch slave traders.

The temporary advantage that trade connections could provide gave rise in the first millennium AD to a series of kingdoms in the region directly south of the Sahara Desert and near the Niger River. Each tended to limit the extent and longevity of the others, as did the only partial incorporation by rulers of populations into a new social formation. Two related phenomena introduced a change of scale around the ninth century: the growth of trade routes across the desert—driven by commerce in gold from mines to the south of this region toward markets in North Africa—and the extension of Islam along these routes as clerics and scholars followed in the footsteps of the traders. By controlling the key nodal points in a lucrative network of trade routes, the rulers of the kingdom of Ghana extended their reach over a large and growing territory and provided strong incentives for local elites and traders to accommodate themselves to the dynasty's power and take advantage of the protection and connections it offered.

The king of Ghana, reported the traveler and geographer al-Bakri in the late eleventh century, was not a Muslim, but Muslim traders—Berber and Sudanese—constituted a strong community around him and literate Muslims served the court. Islam provided a common moral framework as well as a code of laws that helped to develop the relations of trust that facilitated trade. But Islam did not extinguish the variety of religious practices among the pastoralists and farmers of the region, nor did the kings expect that ordinary people would give up their religious practices or village communities. Perhaps fifteen to twenty thousand people lived in the capital, and it commanded agricultural resources—from tribute or the labor of royal slaves—from a large surrounding area. The empire form—in a relatively loose variant—suited the conditions well. Ghana constituted a polity of enormous size, and although its power and that of neighboring polities similarly constituted fluctuated, it exhibited impressive political continuity, from the late eighth to the early thirteenth century.[4]

The importance of Ghana—the pioneer—and the successor empires of the Sahel—Mali and Songhay—to world economic history was considerable. Africa was the major supplier of gold to Europe until the conquests of the Americas brought in new sources in the sixteenth century. Ghana illustrates the importance to political power of controlling external connections. The emperor could ensure his cut in the trade of gold and slaves more readily than the extraction of surplus production from "his" people. He could use the profits of trade to buy slaves, who could fight on his behalf as well as produce. His wealth and military power could attract the support of young men who had become detached from or sought an alternative to their own kinship group.

Because empires left their constituent parts relatively autonomous, they could unravel as quickly as they were put together—and be recombined by new conquerors to build another imperial system. Such a pattern eventually befell Ghana, which was slowly eclipsed in the late thirteenth century by a new imperial formation, Mali. Myth has it that twelve kingdoms ceded their power to the dynasty of Sunjiata to create the Mali Empire. It, like many empires around the world, began as composite, with a ruling dynasty—from the Malinke linguistic/ethnic group in this case—rather than as a unified power structure that extended its domination over space.[5] But its growth and continued strength stemmed from control of trade routes linking Sahelian territories across the desert to North Africa and the Mediterranean world.

Michael Gomez, who has embarked on a reexamination of the Islamic empires of West Africa, points out that Mansa Musa, the young king of Mali at the turn of the fourteenth century, knew about the Almoravid and Almohad empires of North Africa and about the Mamluks who ruled Egypt.[6] The title *mansa* can be translated as emperor. Mali was an empire among empires, a multiethnic polity. The emperor not only distributed the resources of trade and conquest to followers, but put together a power base independent of his own society and especially its elite members. Slaves were crucial to his rule, serving in the palace and administration, including the *farba*, a slave who was the head of the royal household and chief of the other slaves.[7] The seemingly incongruous position of a slave who had been torn away from his community of origin and yet exercised power in the polity of his captor or purchaser was in fact the key to his role in imperial administration, one practiced to a high degree in the earlier Abassid Caliphate and later in many African kingdoms. The slave-administrator had no authority or status other than that derived from the monarch's patronage. Such a situation focused the mind.

Alternate practices of slavery

Mali expected loyalty, tribute, and military service from the communities and territories that had been incorporated into it, but left its provinces
to largely run themselves. Like other empires—from Rome to China—it
pulled in people to work on large-scale state projects. It used externally
derived labor to expand the center's control of agricultural production,
settling slaves in villages to supply the royal granaries. Imperial power
promoted a differentiated society: the royal household with its adminis-
trator-slaves, agricultural slaves, army, occupational castes, peasants.[8]

By the time of Mansa Musa, Mali was defining itself in relation to a
wider Muslim world. But it did so carefully—not imposing Islam upon all
of the many peoples the expanding empire took in. The nexus of trade
and Islam did not simply bolster imperial power. It shaped networks, with
the imperial center initially an essential node, but spreading outward
beyond the political reach of the state, creating secondary centers that
might indeed outlast the state. Here were the origins of the Mandinka
merchant diaspora (described in Chapter 1) as one of the elements of
an African polity that, reaching the West African coast, made contact
with Iberian diasporas and contributed to the origins of the Atlantic
slave trade.

But Mali's emperors were experimenting with various forms of extending
power over space. Abubakari II, at the beginning of the fourteenth century, had tried to launch a fleet into the Atlantic Ocean, but his effort
failed. Mansa Musa turned in a different direction with his famous pilgrimage of 1324–26 across the desert to Egypt and on to Mecca. His ret-
inue included thousands of slaves and marked his place as an important
figure in the Islamic world. Gomez sees this epic journey that some viewed
as a proud marker of the wealth and power of an African empire in ambiguous terms. It showed Mali in a light comparable to other great powers of
its time, a time when western Europe was politically fragmented. But the
very magnificence of Mansa Musa's entourage encouraged those who witnessed it to see West Africa as a land not only of gold, but of slaves. And
the point of Mansa Musa's pilgrimage was not to define his empire as an
autonomous entity but as a part—and a less than equal part—of an Islamic
world whose center lay in Egypt and Arabia.

Mansa Musa was also responsible for the building of the great Friday
mosque in Timbuktu, which was designed by an architect from Andalusia
(the Muslim part of what is now Spain). He sent Malian scholars to study

in Morocco. Timbuktu was not only a trading center, but a center of Islamic learning, a role it continued to play after the decline of Mali as it fell under the domination of Tuareg potentates in the 1430s and again under the subsequent imperial system of Songhay.[9]

As in many empires, succession was a problem, a time when the parts of an empire, linked together by personal as much as institutional ties, could recompose or exit. Mali's longevity was respectable by global standards. It was some 350 years—longer than the existence of the United States for example—but its glory was eclipsed by that of another empire that grew up along its edges, just as Mali had gradually superseded Ghana. As Mali's control over key centers, like Timbuktu, waned, what remained was a Malinke kingdom, and as Nehemia Levtzion puts it, "the traditional particularistic spirit of the Malinke nation triumphed over the universal, supratribal appeal of Islam." But not entirely: Islamic clerics remained at the court and Muslim practices influenced the successor kingdoms and chieftaincies. Islam had taken root in merchant groups and commercial towns across a wide expanse of West Africa.[10]

The torch of Islamic empire was taken up in Songhay. Gomez argues that Songhay's most famous emperor, Sunni Ali (r1464–1492), sought to give a less extroverted orientation to the empire, building inland canals and riverain harbors, putting more emphasis on local beliefs and less on the connection to the central Islamic lands.[11] He speculates that this policy change produced a reaction and that Sunni Ali's death might have been an assassination. Here was a moment when a powerful African polity could have changed its orientation toward the world but did not. One might argue that, in its time, this extroverted approach was the more prudent strategy—playing to the strength of the empire as a nodal point in cross-Saharan relations, something attractive to the empire's intermediaries, who might otherwise have had little reason to sustain such an elaborate infrastructure.[12]

The year of Sunni Ali's death, 1492, is no minor date in the world history of empires. With the defeat that year of the last Islamic polity in Iberia and the expulsion of the Jews, Castile and the other kingdoms that eventually became Spain were in the process of building an empire characterized by its intolerance of diversity. Through the conquest of the Americas, Iberian empires would change the global distribution of power. But no one, in Africa or elsewhere, knew that in 1492. The rulers of Mali and Songhay had been following a pragmatic course. One can suggest a parallel to Mali's brief attempt at maritime empire in the more fully realized effort that took place in Ming China in the fifteenth century. The great admiral Zheng He voyaged as far as East Africa between 1405 and 1433—even before the Portuguese explorers reached that region. But the Ming government put an end to such expeditions and banned Chinese participation in overseas commerce for a time. Why the Ming drew back from the sea is a puzzle, but it highlights the importance of both space and political context for empire-building. European explorers of the fifteenth century departed from the edges of a fragmented continent; their rulers sought sources of revenue and authority outside local and regional power structures. Their land connections to the east were blocked by a polity whose power they could not match, the Ottoman Empire, leaving the sea as the only option for a direct connection to the riches of east and south-east Asia. Chinese rulers did not have a similar economic and political need to leapfrog overseas or to spend the state's resources on a navy. Like the empires of the Sahel, they had the resources and the problems of an empire whose primary focus was the control of land, people, and trade routes across land. If we look at the Sahelian empires as a whole, we find a pattern of relatively long-lasting dynasties able, one after another, to dominate trade routes across the western Sahara from the ninth to the late sixteenth century, during which West Africa was the world's most important exporter of gold. Songhay was a major political force until it was conquered from Morocco in 1591.

Connections across the ocean, not just the desert, could be profitable for African empire builders, especially as Portugal linked up to West African commercial networks in the fifteenth century and began to purchase slaves (Chapter 1). To take a slightly later example, Asante, a kingdom somewhat inland from the coast, expanded in the seventeenth and eighteenth centuries, conquering and incorporating a wide range of societies in its region. Before becoming known as a major slave-exporting kingdom, Asante was an *importer* of slaves, buying them from Portuguese slave traders who obtained them from Central Africa. Its main export at the time was gold, but gold mining was part of a more diversified economy. Trade routes connected the kingdom both to the coast and to the Sahel and Sahara to the north. Slaves made an important contribution to the clearing of forests and the development of an agricultural economy. The absorption of slaves may have contributed to the development of the matrilineal descent groups that were so important to Asante society.

In the eighteenth century, slave exports came to overshadow gold exports; Asante became the supplier of slaves to the notorious castles of the Gold Coast and to the ships coming from several European states that called there. As Asante conquered neighboring kingdoms, it both incorporated them and extended its net still wider to bring in more slaves. Asante kings both sought the cooperation of incorporated elites and made use of young men, detached from more traditional moorings or seeking opportunities, as henchmen. The rulers contained with difficulty tensions among elites jockeying for position and the lower orders of society burdened by wars.[13] In the 1820s, as British power slowly grew along the coast and brought its newfound antislavery zeal to Africa, the Asante king worried that losing the export outlet would make it more difficult to maintain discipline over slaves within Asante. The empire weathered this storm, and it took until the end of the century for Britain to exercise effective control over the Asante realm.[14]

The nineteenth century was a time of empire-building in many parts of Africa. The Islamic empires of the western Sahel in the nineteenth century—Sokoto, Masina, and the empire of El Hadj Umar—were built on the networks of religious elites, traders, and pastoralists that crossed the Sahel. They were constructed not only on such connections, but also on a reformist project—to build a truly Islamic state, adding rigor to the mixes of religious and cultural elements that had characterized Sahelian kingdoms. They conquered non-Islamic societies or societies where—or so the conquering elites claimed—Islam was not rigorous enough, incorporating many slaves and selling others. The Sokoto Caliphate, and the emirates that were formed under its umbrella, went particularly far in employing slaves in positions of authority to create a countervailing source of power to the aristocracy of pastoralist origins that had led the empire-building process. The empire of Samori was less militantly Islamic and more directly a conquest state, but it too was vast and incorporative—so much so that it gave French colonial armies a particularly hard time when they moved into West Africa at century's end.[15]

On the southern end of the continent, the Zulu developed a particularly innovative approach to one of empire's global problems: how to make people with attachments to their own lineages or chiefdoms into loyal servants or soldiers of an empire that was incorporating—often violently—such units. The sudden emergence of this empire has given rise to myths: Zulu, rival African communities, and South Africa whites have generated narratives emphasizing the personal nature of the power of the pioneering king, Shaka, the fierce solidarity of Zulu warriors, and the ruthless nature of Zulu expansion. But recent scholarship is developing a more complex portrayal, one more consistent with the practices of empires worldwide as they try to manage internal and external connections and social differences. In the late eighteenth century, with increasing trade coming in and out of Portuguese-held Delagoa Bay (especially in ivory and to a lesser extent in slaves) as well as the Cape Colony, some chieftaincies were able to accumulate resources, exercise more centralized control, and expand. John Wright refers to the larger chiefdoms as "composite polities," containing people who saw themselves as distinct.[16] In the region that became the nucleus of the Zulu empire, chiefs put together *amabutho*, age sets of young men, commonly glossed as "age regiments." These were fighting units of men who came of age and went through initiation at about the same time. They were defined socially as well as militarily. Chiefs could play amabutho off against their own subjects and deploy them to hunt elephants in order to sell the ivory at coastal ports, fight rival chiefs, and accumulate cattle, whose redistribution attracted more amabutho. Arms and wealth brought in women, who could be distributed to important supporters and eventually to designated amabutho.

Born into a rather small-scale chieftaincy, Shaka worked this system particularly well, exploited divisions in larger rival chieftaincies, and set about conquering—but above all incorporating—an ever larger and more diverse set of chiefdoms. Wright argues that Shaka's accomplishments were as much diplomatic as military and the Zulu kingdom was "an amalgamation of discrete chiefdoms." Only the core of the expanding kingdom identified itself as "Zulu." The Zulu empire, like many others, thrived on the tension between armed young men directly loyal to the king and the incorporation of chieftaincies with their collective ethos.

The Zulu system was replicable, and the propagation of these incorporative innovations sent shock waves across so much of southern Africa. The Ndebele may have caused more havoc than the Zulu in the first half of the nineteenth century. Other kingdoms consolidated in a more defensive manner. All needed to obtain and redistribute enough cattle—the principle form of capital—to keep followers loyal in the face of other would-be kings. With their composite nature, their capacity to control the resources of cattle and trade outlets, and above all their ability to cross-cut kinship groups and coopt chiefdoms into armed units directly loyal to the king, the Zulu and related kingdoms reveal another African variant on the theme of empire. They were a challenge to the growing encroachment of white settlers and eventually British troops over the course of the nineteenth century. It was only on the second try, in 1879, that the British army was able to defeat the Zulu one.[17]

A final example of nineteenth-century empire-building is Ethiopia. Under Menelik, this kingdom with its myths of power extending back to antiquity and a history of periodic expansion and contraction underwent a great period of growth and concentration of power in the middle and late nineteenth century. It drew on connections established overland and through the Red Sea and—using European-type weaponry as well as its own forms of organization—constructed a military apparatus sufficiently powerful to defeat the Italian invasion in 1896, maintaining the independence of Ethiopia until it succumbed forty years later to Mussolini's airplanes and poison gas.[18]

In Africa, as in most of the world, empires mixed coercion and incentives, invidious distinction and incorporation, as they faced the problem of governing people who spoke different languages and exhibited different forms of collective identification. Imperial formations like Ghana, Mali, and Songhay developed long-term strategies for dealing with this problem over a large spatial expanse. At one end of the spectrum, difference could be an ordinary fact of life. People came with different ways of living, different senses of collective selves, and expected to interact with people different from themselves. At the other end, difference was the basis of invidious distinction-making, between those insiders and outsiders, civilized and barbarians, "good Muslims" or "good Christians" and bad pagans, between the autonomous self and the enslaveable other.

Bruce Hall and other scholars have lately made a point that invidious distinction-making is not a uniquely European attribute, but a phenomenon found in a variety of situations, including Sahelian Africa. Through fieldwork among contemporary populations and excavation of Arabic texts from the past, Hall shows that desert groups made over the long term distinctions between themselves—light-skinned, with connections to the Berber populations of North Africa—and "blacks." The distinctions were both phenotypical and cultural, and Hall argues that this combination can be categorized as distinctions of race. He is careful to say that race is itself a variable concept and one has to put as much emphasis on the contents of racial thinking as the label of such thinking as "racial." In some of the cases he studies, race is not simply a matter of skin color, but of patrilineal descent, so two people who look alike might be classified differently depending on the status of their fathers.[19] Such analyses are tricky, for one can easily fall into a *tu quo que* argument: they are just as bad as we are.[20] It is fair enough to point out that race is no more a quintessentially European idea than "tribalism" is quintessentially African, but such an observation only gets us to the beginning of understanding what difference means in any context.

Empires of the past did not efface the cultural variety of Africa. They produced political institutions capable—for better or worse—of coming to grips with difference and doing so over relatively long periods of time. Some polities defined certain peoples as "enslaveable others"; they did so in a context shaped by the availability of outlets for slaves, the limits of exploiting one's "own" people, and the ambitions of would-be rulers. Such distinctions could be undone as well as made, and the boundaries of "peoples" were historical variables, not givens of political action. Empires both emerged and fell apart, and the analytical usefulness of the category is not simply to place territories or peoples into it, but to use the concept to think through the trajectories of political formations and their consequences over time, to encourage an examination of the different ways in which incorporation and differentiation, provincial autonomy and centralized authority are conjugated. I am not trying to pin down characteristics inherent in a form of state, of Islam, of a particular ethnicity, or of Africa. Empires could become forces that any polity or community had to deal with, but they did not define all connections over space; indeed, imperial connections may well have spawned networks that not only crossed imperial lines but could eventually undermine imperial institutions.

We, like Du Bois in 1946, do not need to assert Africa's primal innocence, but to see it as part of the world. This brings us to a decisive intersection in the story of empires in Africa—the advent of European colonization. Did this process mark a new kind of empire history, one making invidious distinction its fundament? Did it define Africans' place in the world in a way that previous imperial projects could not?

There have been two poles in the way colonization has been considered in scholarly circles. One emerged in the 1960s and was given clear expression by the Nigerian historian Jacob Ajayi, who termed colonization an "episode in African history," not necessarily more important than other episodes, located between two periods when African societies were independent of rule by people from outside the continent.[21] The other, coming from both apologists and critics of colonialism, has been to emphasize colonization as an event that overwhelmed Africa, an argument given new life in recent years by the evocation of the word "postcolony" as a sufficient descriptor of everything that befell African societies after colonialism had run its course.[22]

But colonial rule was neither a mere episode nor a total remaking. We do not have to minimize the violence—material and moral—of these years to gain a better understanding of what did and did not happen. One recent tendency has been to stress how colonial rule was actually experienced on the ground, going beyond the abstraction of the "colonial subject" to see what Africans brought to the unequal relationship with colonizers and how they countered many of the latter's more vicious thrusts or found niches in the crevices of colonial power. Another approach derives from the relatively new directions in "imperial" or "colonial" history and emphasizes the limitations and incoherence of nineteenth- and twentieth-century European empires.[23]

French and British empire-builders certainly tried to represent what they were doing as a new form of empire. Paul Leroy-Beaulieu's 1874 book *De la colonisation chez des peuples modernes,* for example, argued that the new colonizers would be engineers and doctors, not conquistadors, and their efforts would benefit both colonizers and colonized.[24] Crusaders against the slave trade in Africa, especially after David Livingstone's account of the depredations of the trade in central Africa, made a case to otherwise skeptical British subjects that a new effort had to be undertaken to bring Christianity, civilization, and commerce to a benighted people.

We need not take colonial ideologues at their word about the originality—let alone the merits—of their project. The reality of conquest bears comparison with the Mongols with new technology—machine gun and telegraph instead of bow and arrow and horse relay teams—a form of conquest based on inflicting terror and moving onward, picking up local troops along the way, rewarding them and leaving in place little in the way of administrative structure. What constituted administration thereafter was authority exercised through intermediaries referred to as "chiefs." Bureaucratic rationality as a mode of governance existed mainly on paper. British and French officials soon realized that projects of remaking Africans were, with the exception of mining zones in southern Africa and some urban areas, too dangerous and too expensive.[25]

Telling the story of the beginning and the end of European colonial empire in Africa will also look different if we tell it as an inter-empire story in a long time frame. Ever since the fall of the Roman Empire, there have been attempts to build an empire on Rome's scale on the European continent and attempts—most effectively by other empires—to block such efforts: the line runs from Charlemagne to Charles V to Napoleon to Hitler. In the early and mid-nineteenth century, British advantages in economic and naval capacity enabled it to deploy a relatively flexible repertoire of power overseas: maintaining tight control over the still-lucrative West Indian colonies while supervising the transition from slave to a mix of indentured and other forms of labor, allowing Canada and other "white" colonies to obtain a new, self-governing status while their populations remained subjects of the king or queen, tightening rule over India, and making ample use of what has been called the "imperialism of free trade"— market relations supported by gunboats—in newly independent South American republics and coastal Africa.[26] Inter-empire competition in and near Europe led to complex alliances and intrigues with and against Russia, the Ottoman empire, and the Habsburgs—in which multiple imperial resources, continental and maritime, were mobilized. Later in the century, as Germany began to catch up with Britain in industrial power, it incorporated French, Danish, and Polish speakers into its empire, challenged Britain on the seas, and developed overseas interests. The nature of imperial competition changed. One can best understand the scramble for Africa as preemptive colonization by competing empires, each trying to prevent others from controlling access to tropical raw materials and markets that had been managed via trade relations with Africans along the coasts for many years.[27]

The Europe-Africa connection was hardly new, but it was becoming more intense as different European powers competed for tropical products, like palm oil, that were becoming vital for European industrialization. The combination of four or five rival European powers seeking connections with African territories that were themselves divided into rival empires, kingdoms, and small-scale polities produced a volatile situation. The danger was that the divisions on European and African sides might give rise to an unstable pattern of alliances excluding others from particular territories. In what is thought to be the first Ph.D. in history written by an African (published in 1956), K. Onwuka Dike described such a scenario in the Niger Delta. Rivalries among Delta "houses" (the kinsmen of a merchant-ruler extended by the incorporation of slaves and clients), tenuous relations of major houses with British merchants, and German-British rivalry over such connections led to a gradual escalation of British intervention and to eventual takeover of the region in order to impose a pax britannica on a situation where British access to palm oil was at risk.[28] Similar situations arose in other areas.

The preemptive nature of the scramble for Africa helps to explain one of the main paradoxes of the first half-century of colonization: why did European powers, whose technological dominance over African societies was so clear and whose racial and cultural arrogance so intense, do so little actually to develop the regions they conquered? European colonization neither systematically remade Africa nor systematically exploited its population. Africans working for wages—however miserable—remained a tiny percentage of the population until after World War II. Little capital was invested except in mining zones, certain areas of white settlement, or port or capital cities. Of the crops that proved among the most useful to Europe, including cocoa and palm oil, African initiative—not the incitement of colonial agents—was largely responsible for their growth. The economics of colonialism were above all the economics of fragmentation: islands of wage labor (or forced labor) surrounded by vast areas whose non-integration in marketed production facilitated the recruitment of cheap labor, but also regions where African farmers attained a modest degree of prosperity, using kinship, clientage, and connections across long distances to recruit labor. South Africa stands out as the place where a particular, racialized variant of proletarianization was carried out, dependent not only on land grabbing, but on a sufficiently dense white population to allow for the policing of migration and the maintenance of discipline on a systematically exploited labor force (Chapter 1).

One can make a related argument about politics and administration. Early on, British and French governments, at least, talked about changing the ways Africans worked and lived, but—given the gap between the vastness of the task and the meagerness of the revenue African colonies seemed likely to produce—they did not give themselves the means to do so. A recent study describes British colonies in Africa as "fiscal and financial backwaters." The Gold Coast and Nigeria derived 60 percent of revenue from customs revenues, most of the rest from hut or poll taxes that required cultivating relationships with chiefs to collect.[29] The colonial establishment was thin: all of British tropical Africa, with more than 43 million people, had fewer administrators in 1939 than the City of Cambridge, Massachusetts, now has employees.[30] Up until 1940 in the British case and 1946 in the French, colonies were expected to be self-sustaining in revenue—they were not supposed to cost the metropolitan taxpayer money, except as an investment consistent with market principles. Colonial governments put modest sums into narrow channels of communication, mainly drainage networks to bring goods—African-produced or from mines or settler farms—to ports. They were setting the precedent for what governments of formerly colonized territories would do after independence—act as gatekeepers at the junction between internal and external economies.

Colonial regimes found they had to rely for revenue, labor mobilization, building roads, and many other governmental actions on the very elites of African societies whom they had disparaged in legitimating conquest. Chiefs, as they usually were called, could be arbitrarily fired, but colonial states ultimately depended on chiefs' retaining a degree of legitimacy, which they could use to defend their communities against the worst of colonial predations or—more likely—to foster their own positions. African historians have brought out the volatility of such relations of power and the fragmentation they enhanced in African societies.[31] They have also spelled out a more complex view of cultural change than some followers of Michel Foucault have presented of colonial power insinuating itself into daily life or of a "colonization of consciousness." African communities built up at mission stations developed a variety of reinterpretations of lessons taught, and often—as in the independent churches of Nigeria or the Kimbanguist movement of the Belgian Congo—asserted complete autonomy from European denominations.[32] This nuanced picture in no way diminishes the racism or brutality of colonial regimes, most obviously in the case of settler societies but also directed against the most "civilized," as colonists would say, of western-educated, mission-trained African elites. The periodic massacres in which colonial regimes indulged were one dimension of their inability to routinize administration. Scholars who like their colonialism very colonial have trouble dealing with the fragmented, uneven, mediocre nature of colonial administrations, as well as the creativity with which African communities reconfigured the structures and ideologies imposed on them.[33]

The most thorny question about colonial situations—as Du Bois well understood—was that of race. Colonized people felt the brunt of racism at several levels, from daily humiliations to the elaboration—from writers like Carlyle or de Gobineau—of theories of human society that put blacks at the bottom. But as scholars look more deeply into the question of racism, it becomes no less vicious but much less coherent. Notions that a "scientific racism," born of classificatory thinking characteristic of the Enlightenment, run into the problem that at no point did scientists agree on the nature and significance of race. Some scientists could follow "reason" to conclude that the world's population was clustered into unequal groups, but others reasoned that human beings were intermixed in a variety of ways and that skin color, intelligence, or other capabilities did not correlate. If in one sense French, British, Portuguese, and other European ideologues of colonialism put together a view of African inferiority more consistent and more fully rationalized than that of past rulers of empire— including those of West African empires—those arguments had to confront an equally coherent counterdiscourse about the scientific baselessness and fundamental inhumanity of racist arguments.[34]

Some of the best historical studies of race put more emphasis on experience of domination than scientific preconceptions. Thomas Holt and Catherine Hall have shown how ex-slaves' refusal to fall politely into the roles assigned to them as wage laborers after the abolition of slavery in British colonies in the 1830s led to a growing conviction that people of African descent were a racial exception to an economic rule.[35] The very fact of colonization led conquerors to justify their actions by evoking the supposed inferiority of people with whom other Europeans had previously traded as autonomous actors. Anxious officials in the twentieth century patrolled the racial frontier, fearing that their claim to authority would be rendered ambiguous by whites who "went native," by racially mixed children, or by not keeping the best educated Africans in their place.[36]

Among colonial officials, missionaries, and economic interests, racial thinking took different forms. The missionary who wanted to save souls and remake African culture in a "Christian" mode and the owner of a mine or plantation who wanted to exploit labor without regard to the humanity of the worker were both thinking in racial terms, but not in the same way or with the same implications for Africans' life chances or for the possibilities for Africans to seize and turn the discourses being imposed on them into claims. Portuguese official policy shifted in the late nineteenth century from an assertion that colonies would constitute "civilizing stations" in Africa to one in which Africans' lack of civilization justified continued use of forced labor. But by the early twentieth century Portugal's forced labor regime became the object of attack by a humanitarian lobby—largely British, heirs to the mantle of the abolitionist movement of the previous century.[37] The Congo of King Leopold II of Belgium also came under fire from the lobby, and these inter-empire publicity campaigns had the effect of distinguishing a colonialism acceptable in European quarters from one that was not, on the basis of how Africans were "treated." The League of Nations in 1926 brought up "conditions analogous to slavery" in European colonies, pointing the way to a notion of legitimate colonial governance quite at variance with actual practices of all the major colonial powers. In British Africa, for example, Africans were frequently coerced into labor on farms and mines—and more were pressured by land alienation and lack of resources into seeking wage labor—giving rise to a dialectic of scandal-making by humanitarians and attempts by officials to disguise the coercive and discriminatory nature of the system. Africans were far from passive object of debate over their treatment in regard to labor and other dimensions of life, through repertoires of protest that included petitions, newspaper articles, mass demonstrations, and strikes as well as myriad individual and collective strategies that made recruitment and discipline more difficult to implement effectively.[38]

Indeed, the most important point is that racialist thinking was continuously contested by Africans and African Americans. The insidious nature of racial classification and discrimination became one of the main points around which the attack on the inhumanity of colonial rule was mobilized. Du Bois enters this picture with his famous dictum of 1903, and West Africans were already arguing against colonial racism, at a time when colonial rule had barely been consolidated.

It was also in 1903 that J. E. Casely Hayford, an African lawyer and journalist from the British Gold Coast, spelled out another important counter to demeaning representations of Africa by patiently explaining African institutions and their potential place in a changing world. In his book *Gold Coast Native Institutions* he analyzed Asante and Fanti institutions of government, showing their potential for the future within a layered system of government—a revealing adaptation of notions of rule that were both imperial and indigenous.[39] Casely Hayford described coastal polities as "federated" unions, whose authority over the component parts was widely accepted. Here is what he said about the provinces within these federations:

> Each of these important communities, in regard to the entire State, was a sort of imperium in imperio—in fact several native states federated together under the same laws, the same customs, the same faith and worship, the people speaking the same language, and all owning allegiance to a paramount king or president, who represented the sovereignty of the entire Union.[40]

He reminded his readers of the attempt by Fanti in the 1870s to write their own constitution, which, if the British had allowed it, would have formalized and adapted existing institutions into a federal state that would be an agent for progress, building schools and roads, and regulating the extensive commerce between the Gold Coast and the outside world. He severely criticized British colonial administration, but he did not seek to overthrow it altogether. He wanted a self-governing Gold Coast—run according to what he termed "aboriginal principles"—to take its place alongside Canada and other territories within a greater Britain, which would both convey and enjoy the benefits of interaction. As a lawyer, he astutely argued that the arrangements he advocated were more in keeping with agreements that British officials had made with African polities over the nineteenth century than the domineering form of rule that was being exercised in 1903. He looked forward to the creation of an "imperial West Africa, with federal Fanti and Ashanti as a basis." In that circumstance, he could imagine "flying the Union Jack, not by coercion in any shape or form, but by free choice, as becomes a free people."[41] Naive one might say—but that would be to project backward a 1960s notion of independence to 1903. Casely Hayford saw federation as a reality rooted in African practices—in African empire, if you will—and sought to transform it by bumping up the federal concept another notch, so that a federal West Africa would become a part of a federal British empire. To make such an argument required a basic assault on British prejudices about African backwardness, and that is what he set out to do in much of his text.

Casely Hayford's ideas reappeared in his own attempt to organize a political party at the level of British West Africa as a whole in the 1920s.

One can see similar reasoning behind the effort by leading politicians in French Africa between 1945 and 1960 to create a West African federation as part of a confederation that would include France and its former colonies (Chapter 3).

Colonial rule became more involute as European powers realized the limits of their power to systematize the exploitation of Africans and as their will to pursue anything like a civilizing mission wavered. When Africans—who died by the thousands for their respective empires during World War I—demanded in its aftermath recognition for having paid the blood tax, including at least some of the rights of citizenship, French and British governments reacted by asserting that such claims went against the authentic traditions of Africans. They posed as the guardians of the diverse cultures of their empires, invoking the doctrine of "indirect rule" in the British case, "association" in the French. In their view, chiefly rule, traditional practices, and the distant protection of civilized powers, not the voice of citizens, was what African politics should be about. But Casely Hayford was by then only one of many African voices—coming from western-educated elites and increasingly from workers, military veterans, and students—claiming a place as citizens of empire. Meanwhile, in Asia, the Middle East, and elsewhere in the colonial world, political activists were not only beginning to speak back to the colonial powers in the language of "self-determination" but were speaking to each other about different ways to combat imperial domination.[42]

During the depression of 1929, the British invoked "imperial preference" to try to keep sterling within the empire, and in order to maintain revenue as export tax receipts declined they forced chiefs to extract more from their people.[43] Wage labor forces in much of Africa were reduced, and the social burden of caring for the jobless was diffused into the African countryside, where the victims of depression would be less visible and less dangerous. There was no lack of conflict—and a notable development along Pan-African, cross-empire critiques of colonialism—but on the ground, colonial regimes were able to take advantage of the fragmentation they had fostered to isolate Pan-Africanists and other elite critics and to keep rural protest in tribal containers.

But the unease was palpable and emerged more clearly in centers of wage labor—notably the Copperbelt of British Central Africa—as the depression eased, more workers were hired, and conditions remained miserable. Major strikes, embracing women and men in the towns and not just individual companies, broke out in 1935 and 1940, as they did in a number of port cities in West and East Africa.

This brings us to World War II, and here we arrive at a break in the history of empire. Du Bois recognized the importance of this juncture. He later noted that because of the depression the Pan-African movement was largely on hold from 1930 to 1945. In 1945, at the Manchester Conference, Pan-Africanists tried to seize the moment. The conference resolutions were a searing indictment of colonialism—for its racist practices and ideologies, for exploitation, for denial of political voice. They pointed to the "democratic nature of the indigenous institutions of the peoples of West Africa." They called for following the principles of the Atlantic Charter, for rights of free speech and assembly, for the end of racially discriminatory practices such as pass systems, and most powerfully for the right to vote and "for the right of colonial peoples to control their own destiny"—to elect their own governments, to organize against imperialist exploitation. The last word of the resolutions was "Unite!"[44]

What the resolution did not make clear is what the unit in which Africans should choose their own governments should be. Territories, as defined by colonial borders? Africa as a whole? West Africa? French or British Africa? An ensemble of people of African descent around the world?

The political context was volatile.[45] Unlike in the aftermath of World War I, the European winners were almost as devastated as the losers. Most important, Japan had for a time gained full or partial control of Dutch Indonesia, French Indochina, British Malaya, and American Philippines. Not only were notions of the invincibility of the white race overturned, but after the war France and the Netherlands had in effect to recolonize their valuable southeast Asian colonies. Nationalist movements under Ho Chi Minh and Sukarno immediately moved into the vacuum of the Japanese defeat. France and the Netherlands were in the end unable to reestablish secure power over Indochina and Indonesia. Nor were the British in a position to renege on their promises to Indian nationalists, as they had after World War I; India and Pakistan became independent in 1947.

Just as important was the shifting situation in western Europe itself. The conflict for dominance that dated to the fall of the Roman empire came to an end. France, Germany, and Britain no longer had to fear each other's supremacy. The two real winners of World War II were the US and the

USSR; they would continue imperial rivalries in new forms. Germany and Japan, defeated as empires, were able to flourish as nation-states. They did not fear any longer that another empire would monopolize resources or markets. The idea of world markets distributing resources around the world made more sense as the big empires were cut down to size, an arrangement that suited the US quite well and to which the USSR posed a radical alternative.

The initial reaction of France and Britain to their loss of Asian territories was not to give up on empire, but to make more of their African colonies. They realized they not only had to get serious at long last about developing their resources, but they also had to find a renewed basis of legitimacy. They sought to meet both ends by embracing the notion of development—more exports to save the franc and the pound by selling African raw materials to the United States and elsewhere and promotion of a higher standard of living for Africans. Africans would be given more political voice, but not too much or too rapidly. The British government abandoned "indirect rule" in favor of "local government," now seeking to coopt the educated Africans whom it had previously looked down upon as not representative of authentic African values. The French government took a step that the British never even considered—allowing a small number of Africans, elected in a limited franchise, to take seats in the legislature in Paris, where they would participate, as a minority, in enacting laws, including the writing of a new constitution for France.

At the end of World War II, both French and British governments formally repudiated race as a legitimate category of state practice with surprising alacrity, sending directives to local administrators to avoid racially discriminatory practices and to pressure European businesses to stop denying service to Africans.[46] The policy change stemmed in part from Hitler's having given racism a bad name and in part from the need to make colonial rule both more productive and legitimate. But they were able to do so quickly and without much agonizing because—as Helen Tilley has emphasized—there was no prior consensus among governing elites and their advisors about the place of race in an imperial order.[47] European administrators did not insist, at this point, that the legitimacy of their rule depended on African inferiority. They also did not realize how volatile the new claims they made to assert their legitimacy through projects of economic development and political inclusion would turn out to be.

The official repudiation of racial justifications for colonial rule did not mean nonracialism in practice. Indeed, whites in the colonies often tried to act as if nothing had changed and official racial discourse itself was to a large extent reconfigured more than eliminated, focused less on Africans in general than on Africans who behaved in certain ways.[48] The revised perspective could mean that the African who refused to conform to the "modern" ways recently made available to him was acting in a willfully destructive manner and deserved the designation of "savage" that reappeared during such events as the Mau Mau Emergency in Kenya or the war in Algeria. White settlers in those contexts used their rights as citizens—and their political connections—to make sure that Africans did not get to exercise whatever new rights they officially acquired.[49]

Both the tensions within Africa and the new configuration of global power implied that the dynamics of political movements would be shaped by the give and take of political struggle—by concessions of the imperial powers and possibilities that opened up, where there seemed a real chance to make claims and perhaps gain a measure of power. Whether a future African nation would be defined by the borders of Nigeria or Senegal, by something like Casely Hayford's federated West Africa, or by a reformed French empire was not clear. We might think, given the tottering state of European power signaled by Du Bois in 1946, that the Pan-African movement would take off from that point. It did not. Politics took another direction.

In the British case, the dynamic was territorial. Kwame Nkrumah, who had been at the Manchester conference, relates in his autobiography that given his Pan-African orientation he had not focused particularly on his native Gold Coast when he returned to Africa and ended up almost by chance back home.[50] That was where the action turned out to be, and Nkrumah plunged into the activities of the United Gold Coast Convention that was trying to mobilize the population, particularly in cities, against colonial rule. A boycott of European businesses in 1948 led the government to make a few concessions, but a march of ex-servicemen—disappointed by the lack of jobs or social services after their tours of duty in some of the most brutal sectors of the war—ended with soldiers under British command shooting at the veterans and killing several. Riots broke out in major cities, and the government alternated repression and concessions.

British attempts to direct educated Africans to local councils in their respective colonies failed quickly, and the battle for power was now at the center of each colony. Nkrumah understood quite well that the British government was in a defensive posture and could no longer force politics back into "tribal" containers. Wage workers, city dwellers caught between heightened economic activity, rising prices, miserable infrastructure, and inadequate commercial facilities, and young men searching for opportunities became key elements of his constituency—a mix officials rightly perceived as dangerous. Pan-Africanism remained in Nkrumah's mind, but for the moment, he was engaged in a struggle that he now had reason to think he might win—for power in the Gold Coast. The British government came to accept that the only antidote to urban disorder was an electoral politics that would give scope to "respectable" political actors who might channel mobilization in an acceptable direction. By 1951, they found that the only actor who had the standing to accomplish such a task was Nkrumah himself.

In the case of French Africa (to be discussed in detail in Chapter 3), the quest for liberation was clear, but not the form it would take. Politicians like Léopold Sédar Senghor of Senegal were thinking in terms of some kind of federalism—looking beyond the individual territory—and, again like Casely Hayford some 40 years earlier, of transforming empire into a consensual union. At the center of such ideas was a claim that had repeatedly surfaced in the history of French colonialism since the revolution in Haiti in 1791—for French citizenship. Senghor gave the argument a particular twist by insisting not just on rights in some abstract sense, but on conjugating Africans' assertion of their own civilization—and he saw it as "Negro-African," not Senegalese—with participation as rights-bearing citizens in a unit that remained French.

This was a reading of the colonial situation that addressed the many dimensions of inequality and humiliation but was more supple than one that posited a sharp separation of elite and subaltern, of colonizer and colonized. It looked not to an immediate reversal of power relations but to a process. It is impossible to adjudicate whether Senghor's dialectic of African solidarity and French citizenship or Frantz Fanon's "the last shall be first"—a rejection of any compromise with colonial authority and the creation of an insistently anti-imperial nation—was the better strategy, except to say that both were readings of colonial situations that corresponded to some of their realities.[51] And each strategy contributed to the other's success, confronting France with the dangers of intransigence and the costs of reform.

What was imaginable in 1946 but not in 1966 was that there were multiple alternatives to empire that did not presume that the end point was the nation-state. Pan-Africanism, certainly in its earlier Du Boisian variant, was one of them—with its notion of a vanguard leading a diasporic collectivity to dismantle the hierarchy of colonialism. Another was federalism, an idea backed by practically all leaders of French West Africa in the 1940s, up to 1958 at least. The 1955 Bandung conference among the heads of newly liberated states postulated a new kind of political arrangement based on the common fact of having been colonized, with relatively unspecified notions of how a Third World would operate.

The argument for self-determination was a powerful language for claiming equality, but the problem was that the "self" that was to do the determining was ambiguous: Asante or Ghanaian?[52] Biafran or Nigerian? African or French? diasporic African or territorial? In 1946, it was not yet the case that political autonomy and belonging to a larger unit were mutually exclusive.

In 1957, the Gold Coast became independent. Nkrumah, the principled critic of empire in his time, must have had a romance of empire in another era, for he chose to name the newly independent country Ghana after an empire conveniently distant—unlike the Asante empire—from the actual experience of his people. Ancient Ghana was located well to the northwest of Nkrumah's Ghana. The ancestors of some of the people living in his Ghana may well have done the hard labor that produced the gold whose commercialization and transportation underwrote the economy of ancient Ghana. Senghor and his fellow leaders made a similar move three years later when they chose to name the new—disappointingly small—federation they had created the Mali Federation.

In 1958, Nkrumah proposed to give up some of the sovereignty his state, through the determination and courage of Ghanaian political activists, had just won. He urged the All African Peoples Conference, held in Ghana's capital, to create a United States of Africa. Du Bois, in a speech that because of his illness his wife presented to the conference, also spoke of the importance of unity, of carrying politics to a higher level. "Your local tribal, much-loved languages must yield to the few world tongues which serve the largest number of people and promote understanding and world literature. This is the great dilemma which faces Africans today, faces one and all: Give up individual rights for the need of Mother Africa; give up tribal independence for the needs of the nation."[53]

Nkrumah's United States of Africa did not turn out to be that nation. Nor did Senghor's vision of a West African federation that would be part of a French confederation. But why were such ideas *imaginable* in 1958? Why did politicians as astute (and different) as Senghor and Nkrumah look beyond territorial nationalism? They had come of political age in a time when empire was still an ordinary part of world politics—as it had been since the days of ancient Ghana—and when the non-equivalence of peoples was enshrined in international law and institutions like the League of Nations. They understood what constituted empire quite well, and they were seeking a route out of it. But they thought there was more than one route, and the territorial nation-state posed dangers as well as embodied aspirations. The success of political movements in Africa after World War II was both a liberation and a narrowing of political imagination and political possibilities.

3

‿o‿

Africa and the Nation-State

From the Manchester Conference of 1945 through Du Bois's *The World and Africa* of 1946 and Aimé Césaire's *Discours sur le colonialisme* of 1950, the indictment of colonialism was strong and clear. Ideas for liberation were many. This chapter focuses on a particular set of African political actors in a particular context: French West Africa between 1945 and 1960.[1]

As late as 1960, most leaders in French West Africa were still seeking alternatives to both the colonialism of the past and what they feared would be the powerlessness of small, impoverished nation-states. They thought that inequality—in wealth and power—was a reality that had to be faced, even as they insisted that all peoples had equal dignity that needed to be recognized. Their arguments have become obscured by the retrospective view that national independence was the only wave of the future. Some leaders of French Africa have been dismissed as having imbibed a "French colonial myth," delaying for some years the inevitable triumph of the nation-state.[2]

One can too easily fall into an "I'm more radical than thou" debate. What course would represent a more profound transformation of the relationship of colonized to colonizer—for political movements to slot themselves into the model of the sovereign, territorially bounded nation-state or for them to insist on transforming the empire itself into an egalitarian polity?[3] Leaders of French Africa in the 1940s faced questions like these

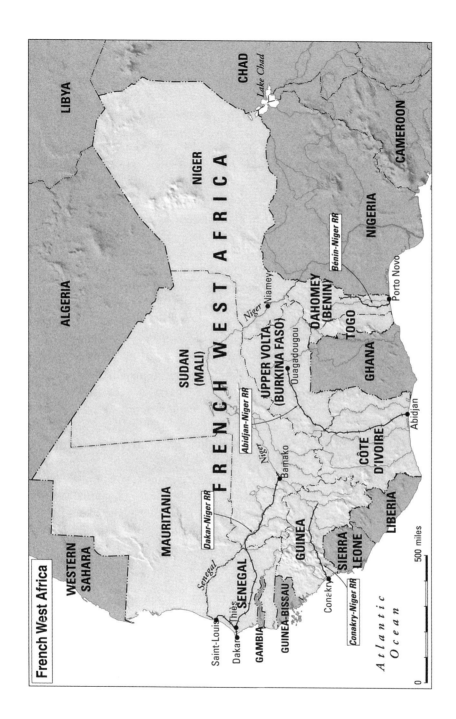

French West Africa

not as abstract political models but as actual choices. Most of them saw the trajectory to the nation-state as leading to "nominal independence" within a world that they insisted was increasingly interdependent. They contrasted such an alternative to "real independence." Rather than see real independence as the attainment of the bounded nation-state, they argued for a more layered approached to sovereignty, balancing territorial autonomy with inclusion in a larger entity. The structure of empire, preserving the distinctiveness of its component parts, could become the starting point for a new type of diverse polity, if it could be stripped of the notion that such parts were arranged hierarchically. Empire would be transformed into federation or confederation (the latter implying a higher degree of national identification and autonomy than the former). Africans did not all agree on how such a goal should be accomplished, nor did leaders in metropolitan France and in African France necessarily see the possibilities of a federal France in the same terms.

Turning colonialism into federalism might be thought to be too utopian a vision or too much of a compromise. But the "realistic" alternative has not proven itself to be such a clear route to human progress. Nor does historical experience suggest that the most "radical" anticolonial movements (Angola, Zimbabwe) did better in leading former colonies to social justice, economic progress, and political democracy than those that attained independence via negotiations and compromise. We know—and the civil war that beset Algeria from the moment of its independence is a case in point—that the very claim by a political party or movement to be the true embodiment of a total reversal of a colonial past can provide a rationale, if not a reason, for new forms of state oppression and violence.[4]

The point is not to say what should have been done, but to recapture the sense of multiple possibilities—and of debate among their advocates—that characterize the years after 1945. The past may not point to a path to the future, but if we are to let our political imagination expand in the future, it is worth remembering that, in the past, there has been more than one way of imagining things.

One of the more self-consciously militant political leaders of French West Africa, Mamadou Dia of Senegal, stated in 1955: "It is necessary in the final analysis that the imperialist concept of the nation-state give way to the modern concept of the multinational state."[5] Mamadou Dia, brought up as a Muslim, trained in French schools to be a teacher, stalwart of the political party led by Léopold Sédar Senghor, future prime minister of

Senegal, was dedicated not only to giving Africans an equal place in the multinational state he advocated, but in using political activism to bring about social and economic equality.[6] Dia was saying that the nation-state was neither modern nor desirable. His views were typical of his time; the only political party of stature in Sub-Saharan French Africa advocating territorial independence before 1958 was in Cameroon. What Dia and other Africans sought was federation, of African states with each other and with France. Their politics was firmly anticolonialist, but it was not nationalist in the conventional, territorially focused sense. They feared the consequences of turning the eight small colonies that made up French West Africa—most resource-poor, all suffering from a colonial legacy of inadequate infrastructure—into eight impoverished, weak nation-states. Dia's Senegalese mentor and colleague Léopold Senghor frequently warned against what he called the "balkanization" of Africa—an analogy to another imperial breakup that had gone wrong—indeed whose effects still resonated in the Balkan wars and ethnic cleansings of the 1990s.

Dia's and Senghor's insights have proven prophetic. Quite conscious that they had few means to meet the many aspirations of the citizen mobilization that had brought African political parties to power, the first generation of rulers of newly independent states by and large tried to use the most important resource they had—sovereignty. Even Senghor became the phenomenon he had earlier warned against, jealously guarding his power as president of a territorially bounded nation-state. But what does it signify to the study of African history and politics that the dangers of territorial politics were recognized and alternatives proposed?

It is easy to ignore or expunge the entire issue. African governments, coming to power, were eager to rewrite their recent histories as the triumph of a national movement and themselves as fathers of the nation, even though such fathers as Senghor and Félix Houphouët-Boigny had until the last moment tried to father something other than the nation-state. France was at least as eager as its former colonies to confine the colonial past to an episode, one that lay outside the republican tradition of government, something that could be neatly bounded and excised from history.[7] Both African and French versions of nationalizing history have in more recent years come under critique, as much because of discontent with the present as because of scholarly curiosity about the past.

We might, however, ask different questions about the present if we think of it as the product of specific historical processes, not inherent conditions or a preset trajectory. Since the mid-1970s, France has been trying to exclude as unwanted *immigrants* the sons and daughters of people whom it was trying in the 1950s to keep, as *citizens,* within the empire. The definition of Frenchness that is involved in today's debate does not go back to 1789, but to the 1960s, when France gave up its attempt to keep Africa and Algeria French. That the inhabitants of French Africa, between 1946 and 1960, had the rights of citizens, without their being assumed to be culturally identical to French people, is conveniently forgotten in talk about citizenship and national identity today. And lest we get too taken up with the inevitability of sovereign nations as units of belonging and action, we should remember that sovereignty has always been a less clear notion in historical reality than it is in theories of international relations and law. In the 1950s, leaders of both African and European France were arguing over just how one could develop a system of divided and layered sovereignty, in which African territories and a Greater France would divide up sovereign functions. France did not in the end agree to do so with its former colonies, but it decided that it wanted the concept of layered sovereignty for itself, and that premise is embodied in the European Union. Keeping in mind these alternative—or perhaps complementary—possibilities might make us pause to think about the Frenchness of France, the Europeanness of Europe, and the Africanness of Africa.[8]

Let us start in 1945—and with the acute uncertainty among French leaders about the future of the French empire, and indeed of France itself. After the defeat at the hands of Germany in 1940 and especially the loss of France's most lucrative overseas territory, Vietnam, to the Japanese, French leaders knew they had to find a way to make empire both more legitimate and more productive. The bitter, and ultimately vain, struggle from 1946 to 1954 to regain control over Vietnam meant that France needed African economic resources all the more. Leaders tried quite self-consciously to construct a more inclusive empire, in which elites from the colonies would have some—but not too much—voice, and they hoped that new initiatives in economic and social development would give most Africans a stake in the imperial system. The French Empire was renamed French Union; colonies became "territoires d'outre-mer"—overseas territories. The territories were part of a multiplex, not dualistic, polity consisting of "old colonies" in the Caribbean, "new colonies" in Africa, Algeria, protectorates like Morocco, and mandates like Cameroon, each of which had a distinct juridical status.

As in most empires, the art of government consisted in large part of being able to shift the balance among the various elements of the repertoire. The abandonment of the once-frank category of "colony" signified the hope that by making the empire less "colonial" it could be more durable. And that hope presented the leaders of African political movements with the possibility for opening wider the cracks that had appeared in the system.

Government leaders agreed that representatives from the colonies would have to help write a new constitution, but their numbers would not be proportional to population. French Africans sent a handful of indigenous deputies, elected in a separate electoral college, to the Assemblée Nationale Constituante (recalling the name of the constitution-writing assembly after the French Revolution of 1789). But even a few Africans in the assembly, which also acted as a legislature, were enough to drive such durable, oppressive institutions as forced labor and the *indigénat* (separate administrative justice) out of existence. Senegalese deputies Léopold Sédar Senghor and Lamine Guèye helped draft constitutional articles concerning the French Union. What they sought above all else was to turn colonial subjects into French citizens, with all the rights of the European French person, and hence a platform from which to make further claims. And they wanted something more: for citizenship to be independent of an individual's personal status: a person's civil affairs—marriage, filiation, and inheritance—would not have to come under the French Civil Code but would be adjudicated under Islamic or "customary" law.

Up to then, most colonial inhabitants were French nationals and French subjects but not citizens, and French jurists argued that it was personal status, not race or religion, that was the basis for treating Africans or Algerians as distinct from other French people.[9] To many in the French elite, French citizens were supposed to be equivalent to one another; anything else would recall the distinctions among "estates" that the Revolution had abolished. But it took from 1789 to 1944 for citizenship to be translated into the right to vote for French women, and the revolutionary assemblies had kept changing their mind about the application of citizenship to overseas France, particularly to the slave colony of Saint-Domingue. They had, for pragmatic—threat of royalist reaction, foreign invasion, and slave rebellion—as well as principled reasons, abolished slavery in Saint-Domingue in 1793 and declared ex-slaves to be citizens. But Napoleon tried to restore slavery in 1802, and the Saint-Domingue insurrection turned from an attempt to remake empire into a successful fight to exit from it. Elsewhere, slaves were only freed—and turned into citizens—in 1848. The conquests of Algeria after 1830 and Sub-Saharan Africa (and Indochina) later in the century had brought new peoples into the category of subject.

The Quatre Communes (Four Towns) of Senegal were the major exception to this rule. Small trading enclaves under French rule since the eighteenth century, they depended for security and prosperity on close relations between a tiny population of metropolitan origin and local elites, some of mixed French-African origin, mostly Muslim, who themselves had a variety of connections to the interior of Africa. From 1848 the *originaires,* as they were called, of the Quatres Communes acquired the right to vote (for deputies to the French legislature as well as local officials), although it was in dispute whether they were "citizens" or "voters." What was clear was that the political rights of the *originaires* were independent of the French civil code. Marriage, inheritance, and other family and civil matters came under the jurisdiction of Islamic courts. As Mamadou Diouf has argued, the *originaires* were able to use their rights to defend the particularity of their own religious and cultural community.[10]

When during World War I France needed its African population for defense of the empire, the deputy of the Quatres Communes in the French legislature, Blaise Diagne, negotiated a deal: the French government would affirm that the *originaires* indeed were French citizens—even without coming under the civil code—while Diagne would help organize military recruitment. Similar proposals were made to extend citizenship without change of personal status regime to Algerians, but—with a much larger population at stake and a more powerful lobby of "French" settlers in place—such initiatives failed. They were, however, within the realm of political imagination.

In the Assemblée Nationale Constituante of 1945–46, Senghor and Lamine Guèye argued for the Senegalese system to be generalized across all the territories, insisting that the people whom France considered to be living under its flag could be both equal and different. In introducing such a measure to the constitutional assembly, Senghor cited the heritage of the French Revolution. The Republic, he reminded his colleagues, had in 1793 made the slaves of Saint-Domingue into citizens. He deplored Napoleon's restoration of slavery. Senghor applauded the new revolutionary government of 1848 for at last freeing the slaves definitively and turning them into citizens. At that time, French tradition allowed for no alternative but to assimilate new citizens to the same juridical status as old ones. But since then, Senghor asserted, the Jacobin tradition had been softened by increasing knowledge of sociology and especially ethnography, recognizing the diverse contributions to world civilization of the Arabs, Chinese, Indochinese, and Africans. So now the goal was to recognize both diversity and equality within the French Union, allowing people to come under different legal regimes to regulate marriage and inheritance while assuring everyone equal rights.[11]

There ensued a vigorous debate in the assembly during which emerged French anxieties about being submerged in a sea of indigenous people and questions about how far a republic could recognize differences within its population. Some insisted that Africans were too backward to act as citizens—and they were too numerous to be allowed an equal vote. Others argued that the only way to save the empire, if not France itself, was to assure all its peoples of their full place within it. The debate went back and forth. When it appeared as if the inclusive version of citizenship would be scrapped in favor of a second-order citizenship with unclear implications, most deputies from the colonies followed Senghor and Lamine Guèye in walking out of the assembly. Their exit caused consternation, for most legislators were savvy enough to realize that without at least the acquiescence of the deputies from the colonies, the constitution would have no legitimacy overseas. In the end, most of the provisions of the constitution were compromises: a limited franchise overseas, reserved legislative seats for European minorities in the colonies, and assurance of the sovereignty of the national assembly in Paris over the assemblies in each territory. But the African deputies won their bottom-line demand—the generalization of citizenship, without requiring that the "citizens of 1946"—those from the overseas territories—come under the Civil Code.[12]

This provision did not translate into universal suffrage for another decade. But it conveyed the rights of the constitution to people in the empire, and its language of equivalence quickly proved a springboard for claims to give substance to its terms. In the Overseas Ministry's own interpretation of the articles on citizenship, "the legislature wanted to mark the perfect equality of all in public life, but not the perfect identity of the French of the metropole and the overseas French."[13] In principle, the new French Union would be multicultural as well as egalitarian.

But how far could the French government go in the direction of political equality and still retain both the usefulness of the overseas territories for

French interests and the French elite's tutorial sense, their belief that they knew how to bring people along the road to progress? Unlike empires of the past—which from Rome to the Austro-Hungarians had incorporated people of different ethnicities, civilizations, or nationalities into gradations of status within an inclusive, albeit coercive, polity—citizenship in a European empire would now entail economic and social rights as well as political ones. The consolidation of the welfare state after the war implied growing expectations that the state would guarantee, in some form, citizens' access to pensions, family allowances, health care, and education. If older empires had emphasized hierarchical social order, the French republic proclaimed norms of equivalence of all citizens. Bringing millions of impoverished subjects into citizenship in the 1940s could thus entail high costs—if claims based on contemporary standards of citizenship were made good. And it was not clear that citizens of either European or African France could quickly set aside habits and expectations of privilege and authority, of discrimination and denigration, built up in decades of colonial rule.

These questions were at the heart of political mobilization for the next decade: electoral campaigns in Africa and efforts by deputies in Paris to obtain universal suffrage, the end of protected seats for Europeans overseas, and fuller legislative and executive authority for each African territory. Influential leaders like Senghor pressed their layered approach to political power: each territory would run its internal affairs; French West Africa, heretofore an administrative unit conducive to centralized control, would acquire legislative and executive authority. It would become a "primary federation" that would represent the fundamental unity of African peoples, and this federation would in turn be part of a French confederation. That confederation would exercise power only in specified domains, including foreign affairs and defense, but would also pool resources for common benefit, particularly of resource-poor territories. Senghor argued for combining horizontal and vertical solidarities, horizontal among Africans and vertical with France. Horizontal solidarity without vertical, he insisted, would constitute unity in poverty and weakness, while vertical solidarity without horizontal would be the old colonialism reincarnated.[14]

Senghor explicitly and repeatedly asserted the importance of an African personality, while refusing a bounded, territorial nationalism. In 1949 he wrote on behalf of his political party, the Bloc Démocratique Sénégalais (BDS), "indigenous nationalism" is "like an old hunting rifle." This critique of nationalism led him to his central theme: "Yes, it is good that the Constitution of the French Union allows us to help ourselves with the experience and resources of France, to develop at the same time, with our economic potential, our own Negro-African personality." Such a vision, he insisted, was consistent with the constitution's insistence on equality of race and religion: "We are no more racist than regionalist or nationalist. The BDS in defending the Senegalese and African man defends the man of the French Union and the universal man . . . The 'Human Condition' remains our definitive objective."[15]

Senghor made clear that he wanted to use the power and influence that African political movements could obtain to build a more just social order, a socialist Africa:

> We want less to rid ourselves of the tutelage of the metropole than of the tyranny of international capitalism. We think that an autonomy that simply brings us back to the feudal regime of castes would not solve the problem. We are not rebels, but revolutionaries. We want to construct a better world, better than the colonial world of yesterday, better as well than our world before the European conquest. We will build it taking inspiration from European socialism and the old African collectivism. We will thus reconcile modern technique and African humanism. For it is a question of building a new world where, in an organized society, men will be equal and fraternal "without distinction of race or religion."[16]

Senghor's claims to escape international capitalism and build socialism were softened by his evocation of African humanism and French fraternalism, while his positive, rather homogenized view of a "Negro-African" civilization was sharpened by his rejection of African caste systems and feudalism and his refusal to recreate the African world before the French conquest. But social and economic progress, he emphasized, was better obtained by empowering Africans within the French Union than by a go-it-alone strategy for his small territory.

His party associated with other African parties in the Mouvement des Indépendants de l'Outre-Mer, which staked out a similar position repeatedly from 1948 into the early 1950s. It called for political emancipation and "economic and social democracy," adding a warning that the "temptation of narrow nationalisms represent a grave danger in a world in which independence risks being only an illusion."[17]

The other most influential political movement in French West Africa took a similar position on the relationship of liberation, independence, and the French Union. The Rassemblement Démocratique Africain combined political parties in individual territories into a larger organization whose unity expressed its orientation toward French Africa as a whole. Its founding manifesto, from the fall of 1946, proclaimed, "We have taken care to avoid equivocation and not to confuse PROGRESSIVE BUT RAPID AUTONOMY within the framework of the French Union with separatism, that is immediate, brutal, total independence. Doing politics, do not forget, is above all to reject chimeras, however seductive they may be and to have the courage to affront hard realities." Insisting on working within the French Union, the founding delegates expressed "the certitude that despite reaction, we will obtain the liberal, democratic, and human conditions that will allow the free development of the original possibilities of African genius." The manifesto concluded, "Vive l'Afrique Noire, Vive l'Union Française des Peuples Démocratiques."[18]

In one sense, African political leaders were using the citizenship idea—the sense of belonging to a polity, the combination of the rights of the individual and duties to the collectivity—to make claims on the state. In another sense, they were adapting such abstract notions to their own social and political situations. Senegal represents a striking instance of the turns such a process could take. Although Lamine Guèye was one of the authors of the citizenship provisions of the French constitution of 1946, he was not as quick to grasp its implications as his protégée and fellow deputy Léopold Senghor. Coming from the Quatres Communes, Lamine Guèye's political organization and worldview were shaped by the long experience of those areas with citizenship and with the social structure of the Communes, with their prominent Muslim families. Senghor, born a French subject in rural Senegal, had passed through the narrow door by which individual subjects—through educational credentials and the support of French administrators—had to go to obtain citizenship rights. He understood that the 1946 constitution would soon translate into a large expansion of the voting population beyond the *originaires* of the Quatres Communes.

When in 1948 he set out on his own political path and broke with his mentor, he realized that his best strategy was to make the citizens of 1946 into his constituency. In the manner of skilled politicians around the world, he approached the "people" not as a singular mass but through intermediaries, as members of collectivities. In rural Senegal, the key to doing so was to work through *marabouts,* local Muslim elites who were part of hierarchically organized Islamic brotherhoods, especially the Mourides. Although himself a Catholic, he cultivated his relationship with the hierarchy of *marabouts,* and the support of their followers tipped the political balance of his new party over the Socialist Party of Lamine Guèye.[19]

Political leaders in post-war French West Africa mobilized social ties in different ways. Houphouët-Boigny's start in politics came through his organizing the Société Agricole Africain, based on cocoa farmers, beginning with but not limited to the Baulé region from which he came. When he persuaded fellow deputies in the Assemblée Nationale Constituante to support his proposed bill abolishing forced labor—passed in April 1946— he was not only saving thousands of Africans from being compelled by French administrators and African chiefs to perform stints of poorly paid wage labor for white farmers, but was giving the African pioneers of cocoa production a chance to obtain labor for their own farms. The Société became the nucleus of the Parti Démocratique de la Côte d'Ivoire, branch of the Rassemblement Démocratique Africain. The PDCI-RDA took off from Houphouët-Boigny's emancipatory projects and the networks established during this process that connected workers from the northern part of the territory (and neighboring Sudan and Upper Volta) to the rich agricultural zone to the south.[20]

In the case of Guinea, Sékou Touré built on a trade union base and the reputation he gained as a militant strike leader and organizer in the early 1950s. From there, he extended his political network into the countryside, gaining traction in some areas from grievances against the self-aggrandizing and often oppressive behavior of chiefs associated with the French administration. In the process, he largely abandoned his early politics of "class struggle" in favor of broader appeals to African solidarity against French and aristocratic power.[21]

Politics in the post-war decade thus built on the slowly increasing franchise and the incorporation into a political process of people coming from different kinds of communities across French Africa.[22] Politics also entailed a social struggle, carried out through extensive labor organizing and a series of large-scale strikes in Africa, with increasing support from African political leaders, aimed at making social citizenship into a reality. "Equal pay for equal work" was the slogan of the labor movement, a rhetoric that presumed a continuing imperial connection, for French wage levels and benefits were the reference points for demands for equality.

Beginning with a long general strike in Senegal in 1946, passing through the five-month-long railway strike across all of French West Africa in 1947–48, these movements resulted in substantial gains for wage workers, in the formal sense of the term, including higher minimum wages for ordinary laborers and family allowances for all public employees.[23] In 1952, the French legislature voted—with African unions threatening strike action if they did not get their way—for a labor code that inscribed equal pay for equal work into law and included paid vacations, the right to organize and strike, and other provisions characteristic of post-World War II industrial relations in Europe. In 1956, the overseas public sector's system of family allowances was generalized to the private sector. Related demands were coming from farmers and students, and French officials feared a spiral of demands in the name of the equality of the citizen.[24]

By the mid-1950s, French officials were pulling away from their insistence on central control over policy, realizing that it implied the centralizing of demands for social equality, when economic development was turning out to be a slow and long-term process. But the only way they could hope to get African leaders to back off their quest for equality with metropolitan France was to give them real power at the territorial level.

In the case of French West Africa, the post-war French governments proved capable of calm debate with political activists. Africans could sit in the French legislature, and African labor unions could organize, strike, and claim more equitable pay and benefits. But if the political confrontation strayed beyond certain—unclear—boundaries, the French government was capable of brutal repressive action, and the old colonial tendency to treat an entire category of people as a menace appeared just beneath the surface of post-war politics. Such was the case with the revolt in Madagascar in 1947, the Algerian war of 1954–62, and the suppression of the Union des Populations du Cameroun after 1955. French forces used collective terror against categories of people among whom rebels were supposed to lurk, and they used torture.[25] But even in Algeria, French governments tried programs of "promotion spéciale"—what Americans would call affirmative action—to get Muslim Algerians to see the benefits of inclusion in the French polity.[26]

In French West Africa, the French government handled things more gingerly. For a time in the late 1940s, officials harassed and threatened to ban the Côte d'Ivoire branch of the Rassemblement Démocratique Africain when it both developed a formal relationship of cooperation with the Communist Party in the French legislature and—more dangerous— became so strong in certain rural districts of the Côte d'Ivoire that local officials perceived it to be a second government. But precisely for the latter reason, the administration was not able to undermine it, and in 1950 its leader, Houphouët-Boigny, negotiated a deal to abandon its never very intimate tie to the Communists in Paris in exchange for lifting the repressive efforts.[27] In this way, both France and an African political party made clear the limits of each other's power: France could bar some movements, but not all of those it did not like. African deputies in the French legislature and unions in Africa continued to make their claims and at times—as with the labor code of 1952—got much of what they wanted.

By the mid-1950s, French governments were aware that they were caught in a trap between following through on the logic of citizenship— which was costly—and a cycle of rebellion and repression, now taking place under the gaze of international institutions and observers increasingly skeptical of the normality of colonial rule. The media, as well as government officials, began to consider openly whether preserving an empire of citizens might be less in the interest of France than devolving power and renouncing responsibility.

That was the point of the *loi-cadre* (framework law) of 1956. Rather than revising its constitution to meet demands for systematic rethinking of the organization of the French Union, the government sought to reform the way its African territories were governed, devolving substantial power for internal self-government to elected legislatures and ministers chosen by those legislatures in each of the territories—Senegal, Côte d'Ivoire, Dahomey, and so on. Most African deputies voted for the loi-cadre because it included their major demands for universal suffrage and executive and legislative power for territorial governments, which everybody understood would be chosen by an African majority.

The power conceded in 1956 was real, but it turned out to be a Faustian bargain. African political movements—for whom elections had been a focus since 1945—now acquired a stronger vested interest in the territorial units: patronage to distribute, resources to allocate. The loi-cadre, Senghor feared, would decide the debate over federation and confederation before it was fully engaged. Mamadou Dia later spoke of his "profound and sad conviction of committing one of those major historical errors that can inflect the destiny of a people. . . . In spite of us, West Africa was balkanized, cut into fragments."[28] But Dia and Senghor struggled onward, insisting on the need for a three-level structure right up to the middle of 1960.

Reading speeches and correspondence by French administrators from the late 1940s and 1950s, one comes to realize that a work of imagination was going on—far from achieved—in the official minds of French imperialism. If classic imperial strategies of working through intermediaries— chiefs as they were called in Africa—had underscored both the specificity and the backwardness of African societies, the post-war leap of faith was both an embrace of potential equality and a refusal of particularity. The African worker or farmer would be like a worker or farmer anywhere. The African who could sit in the legislature in Paris was fine; the fact that political parties were making an effort to mobilize peasants was a cause for concern.

In French Africa, the quest for a federal and confederal system continued. Dia and Senghor sometimes referred to the US, the USSR, the British Commonwealth, and Switzerland in seeking to show that what they sought was not unprecedented. They had in mind another sequence than that of empire to nation, mainly that of empire to federation. And in this argument, part of the historical experience of empire—a large entity that was both incorporative and differentiating, that preserved and reproduced cultural difference and sentiments of affinity among its component parts—remained a point of departure, as long as the principle of equality could be assured throughout the polity.

Even Sékou Touré of Guinea, who would break ranks in favor for independence in August 1958, said the previous year:

> We are decided to build the Franco-African Community, while maintaining the unity of Africa which is dear to it. . . . The metropole and the overseas territories should become a grand FEDERAL STATE, including a FEDERAL PARLIAMENT, a FEDERAL GOVERNMENT and AUTONOMOUS GOVERNMENTS.

He made clear that the relations between territories and France "will be on an egalitarian basis or they will not be." And as for French Africa, it was an entity unto itself: "There is no Guinean market, no Senegalese market, no

Ivorian market, but an African market, common to all the African territories of French influence."[29]

But African politicians did not agree on how to federate among themselves. Senghor and Sékou Touré had a strong opponent in Félix Houphouët-
Boigny of the Côte d'Ivoire, who declared that the West African federation
was a "useless and burdensome relay" between African territories and
Paris. He sought a direct relation between territories like his own and the
French federation, in which France would participate in legislative and
executive institutions alongside its former colonies. Although the relative
affluence of the Côte d'Ivoire was a major factor in his thinking—an
African federation would have distributed resources from the richest to
the poorest of the African territories—Houphouët-Boigny was not a
narrow territorialist. He recognized that the economic development of
Côte d'Ivoire depended on labor from poorer territories to the north and
was willing to include migrants within a broad conception of who was
Ivorian. And he was as much an advocate of a multinational polity as
Senghor, Dia, or Sékou Touré: "We are among many who want to reconcile
the life of our states and their personalities with the Community itself. It
is a question of a marriage of both convenience and love. I believe in it;
that is why we remain partisans of the term multinational state."[30]

The 1958 constitution—after Charles de Gaulle came to power in
France in the midst of the Algerian crisis—promoted former colonies from
the status of "Overseas Territories" of the French Union to "Member States"
of the French Community, as the French Union was renamed. The vote in
Africa on ratifying the constitution was a complex affair. In Niger, where
the campaign was the least one-sided, French officials played hard and
dirty against the faction that opposed the constitution—with success.[31]
Elsewhere, lopsided votes revealed the extent to which political parties
had actually developed an apparatus capable of getting out voters and had
managed to exclude alternative political parties from effective competition. France could do nothing to prevent Sékou Touré's party from getting
a suspiciously high 94 percent of the vote against de Gaulle's constitution,
whereas other leaders got similarly suspicious votes for the other side.
Sékou Touré's decision to go against the 1958 constitution came over his
disagreement with de Gaulle about the form that the French Community
would take; some argue it was mostly about a clash of egos, others that
Sékou Touré was pushed by the radicalization of his own party.[32] Be that
as it may, his party, like those who favored the constitution, proved very

good at getting its way. The irony of Sékou Touré's taking a stance at variance with that of most of his fellow politicians was that it made the goal that was dear to his heart—African unity—much more difficult to attain.

The debate over an African federation was high on the political agenda after 1958. Houphouët-Boigny twisted the arms of leaders of other territories who were thinking of joining Senghor, Dia, and Modibo Keita of the French Sudan in creating the African federation. The elites of Dahomey and Upper Volta were very split over this issue. The advocates of African federation were able, in the end, to put together only a truncated association of two states, Senegal and the Sudan, which became the Mali Federation in 1959. Mali became part of a three-tiered structure with "competencies" divided among them: Senegal/Sudan, the Mali Federation, and the French Community. Houphouët-Boigny created a looser rival form of alliance, the Conseil de l'Entente, linking Côte d'Ivoire to Dahomey, Niger, and Upper Volta.

A federation of two was a shaky proposition, but Mamadou Dia embraced it with fervor: "That is how Mali will build itself, and how we can best demonstrate our consciousness, our Malian national will; I do not say Senegalese or Sudanese, because there cannot be a nation at the level of our states—I say our Malian will, and we have the steady conviction that the cause which we serve is the Malian cause, and through it the cause of Africa."[33] It was Mali, not Senegal or Sudan, that would negotiate with France for independence.

In 1959, African leaders made clear that while they insisted on having the rights of French citizenship throughout the Community, they did not accept the idea that the only nationality in the Community was the French one. De Gaulle eventually recognized that they had a point. The French government conceded, in December 1959, that Member States could have their own nationalities and their own mechanisms for deciding who possessed those nationalities. Such decisions would automatically confer the "superposed" nationality of the French Republic and of the Community. In short, a bureaucrat in Abidjan could decide who could exercise the rights of the French citizen, in Dakar or Paris as well as in the Côte d'Ivoire itself. That is how far de Gaulle was willing to go to appease African leaders and keep their territories in the Community.[34]

But when Africans could not agree among themselves where the nation was to lie, each began to see its possibilities in a bilateral negotiation with France. Politicians were already focusing on their territorial bases, and territorial autonomy had distanced the Member States from treating France as the only relevant unit for social and economic claim-making. Rather than concede to each other, first the Senghor faction (Mali) and then the Houphouët-Boigny faction (the members of the Conseil de l'Entente) began to negotiate with France over independence, and France was willing to change the rules yet again to allow independent states to remain within the French Community. Some high-ranking French officials admitted—in the privacy of internal correspondence—that the best hope for preserving the French Community lay with Mamadou Dia, whose firm commitment to African unity and a continued relationship of Africa with France was needed, even if his commitment to social reform caused anxiety.[35]

In August 1960, two months after Mali became independent, the conflict over territorial bases, as well as style of leadership, between Senghor and Dia on the one hand and Modibo Keita on the other became so severe that the federation split up in anger into its component parts, the Republic of Senegal and the Republic of Mali, the former Sudan, keeping the federation's name for itself.[36] Coming after the split between Mali and the Conseil de l'Entente, the breakup of the Mali Federation meant that there was no will to preserve the Community as a collective entity. The hopes of de Gaulle's government in Mamadou Dia's vision of the future could not be sustained. That is how, in 1960, the former colonies of French Africa ended up as a series of nation-states, a goal that neither African nor French leaders had sought in 1945 and that all but Guinea had rejected in 1958.

Senghor's fears of "balkanization" proved only too correct. Each state came under the rule of a political apparatus focused on maintaining control of a territorial structure. The Mali Federation tried to overcome the obstacle that territorial politics had posed since 1956. It failed. There were some attempts after the failure of Mali, including some between anglophone and francophone countries to federate, but they did not come to fruition. Such efforts ran into the attachment of elites to what Africans had really won: sovereignty.

The main protagonists of this story were all caught up in the consequences of the nation-state framework that none of them had earlier favored. Sékou Touré led Guinea to a sudden independence after his successful campaign for a "no" vote on the constitution of 1958. France spitefully cut off most ties. Sékou Touré quickly showed authoritarian tendencies, repressing dissent and organization that he did not directly control, starting with trade unions, whose potential for making claims he understood quite well from his own earlier success in leading Guinea's trade union movement. His repression of a teachers' strike signaled the new order, but not without warning from other leaders, notably Guinea's other trade union figure, David Soumah:

> Unity for unity's sake makes no sense. And a unity which stifles the voice of free trade unionism sets back the emancipation of the laboring masses instead of facilitating it. A unity which ends up in reality in subordinating trade union action to the good will of governments and employers, which submits trade unionism, the very expression of liberty, to a too narrow obedience toward political parties and political men, neutralizes the action of the masses for social progress.[37]

But Sékou Touré was intent on preventing challenges to the asset he controlled, his position as head of a nation-state. And despite the sharpness of its break with France—and its attempts to forge alliances with other African leaders on the radical end of the spectrum and with the Soviet bloc—Guinea was not above doing business with transnational, largely American-based aluminum companies who sought a major place in the country's leading extractive industry. Guinea, for all its mineral and agricultural resources, would remain a poor as well as oppressive country.

Houphouët-Boigny had opposed Sékou Touré and Senghor on the question of an African federation, and his relations with the French government seemed to be as positive as Sékou Touré's were negative. He was a minister of de Gaulle's government and had been on one of the committees that had helped to write the 1958 constitution. But in 1958–60, things did not stay the way they seemed.

When the Mali Federation in late 1959 opened negotiations with France for independence within the French Community via the transfer of "competencies" to the Federation, Houphouët-Boigny was taken aback. What drove him to despair was de Gaulle's positive response to Mali's demands. Despite his own ties to de Gaulle's government, it was Senghor's African federation—even in truncated form—that was advancing with de Gaulle's backing, while Houphouët-Boigny's Franco-African federation was sidelined. Houphouët-Boigny soon upped the ante, asking for independence too and persuading his closest African allies in Dahomey, Upper Volta, and Niger, loosely affiliated in the Conseil de l'Entente, to follow suit.[38] This move accelerated former French West Africa's ride to the nation-state. That ride came to its conclusion by the end of August 1960, as the Conseil de l'Entente states celebrated their individual independences and the Mali Federation split apart.

But Houphouët-Boigny sought for a time to widen the path he had helped to narrow. He proposed flexible versions of citizenship to his nation and those of the Conseil de l'Entente: people from the allied states should have the same rights in Côte d'Ivoire as an Ivorian national as long as that person was in that territory—giving up those rights as soon as he/she left—or else a nationality of the Conseil de l'Entente should be "superposed" on top of the territorially defined nationality (of Upper Volta, Dahomey, etc.) that the individual possessed. Despite the authority Houphouët-Boigny commanded, he could not impose his will on fellow Ivorians who defended a more exclusive notion of Ivorian citizenship. Reducing competition for jobs from people now considered to be non-Ivorian was clearly a major factor behind opposition to these supple versions of citizenship.

Houphouët-Boigny, in any case, consolidated national power in his own hands: he remained head of state for 33 years until his death, and he did little to prepare an orderly succession. After the passing of the man who put together a diverse coalition, the politics of ethnic identification polarized, particularly between south and north. Northerners, especially Muslims, were accused of divided loyalties with neighboring states. The concept of "ivoirité" became the watchword of the exclusivist faction—the ideology of national identification carried as far as attempts to exclude people born and raised within the country but whose parents came from a neighboring state from election to office or even from the vote. Civil war was the result.[39] When a "northerner," Alessane Ouattara, won elections held under international pressure in 2010, the incumbent Laurent Gbagbo refused to accept the results and the conflict entered a new phase of violent conflict, ending only when the intervention of African forces from outside the country and from France put Ouattara into power. Carrying the logic of the nation-state to this level had devastating consequences for the Côte d'Ivoire.

Independent Senegal hesitated between a radical restructuring of its economy and the fruits of a positive relationship with France. But the most serious tension emerged between the quest for socialist-oriented reform—pushed especially by Mamadou Dia—and the electoral machine that Léopold Senghor had built in rural Senegal. Dia wanted to reform the marketing and support mechanisms for agricultural production, running afoul of the well-connected *marabouts* who exercised substantial control over cultivators and traders. Senghor and Dia came into direct conflict within two years of independence, and in 1962 each accused the other of trying to foment a coup. Senghor, with the support of the military, prevailed, and his great comrade and supporter of the 1950s spent the next twelve years in prison. Senghor suppressed all rival political parties.[40] He eventually repented, allowing multiple parties back into the picture, and later—a rarity among African presidents—retired voluntarily from office. Senegal became one of the better African models of multiparty democracy, with incumbents losing presidential elections in 2000 and 2012. But Senghor, in 1962, had come to embody the danger he had predicted from the "balkanization" of Africa: that devolving power to small territories would lead to dangerous conflict for the one resource that mattered, control over the mechanisms of state power.

The ill fit of nation and state still bedevils Senegal's erstwhile partner in federation, the Republic of Mali. In the aftermath of the breakup of the Mali Federation in August 1960, Modibo Keita strove to build a centralized, socialist state. He sought foreign aid from the eastern bloc and tried, without much success, to establish alliances with other radical African states. His autocratic approach did not produce the improvement in living standards of peasants and workers he had promised and alienated much of the population. He was overthrown by a military coup in 1968, and the generals ruled for more than twenty years. But after street protests in 1991, Mali's rulers allowed a national conference, with representatives of different elements of society, to set out a map toward constitutional change. Reasonably free elections were held, and Alpha Konaré, a historian, served two terms as president and duly passed on the torch to Amadou Toumani Touré (a former general reincarnated as a civilian). Touré's reign was marked by accusations of corruption and incompetence, but he seemed to be on the verge of an honorable retirement when in March 2012 younger military officers overthrew him, much to the dismay of Malians, who saw themselves as an example of turn-of-the-century democratization in Africa.

Behind the coup lay a problem that none of Mali's governments since independence had been able to solve: fitting different peoples, some mobile, some sedentary, into fixed borders. Most Malians are Muslim, but that does not fully unify them, for the highly mobile Tuareg of the north distinguish themselves from the largely agriculturalist peoples to the south. Bruce Hall has argued that light-skinned Tuareg have long seen themselves as not only linguistically and culturally distinct from black Africans but a different people, a different race. Some Tuareg have incorporated themselves more fully than others into relationships with the state of Mali and with southern Malians, but many others believe that the state and their non-Tuareg fellow citizens do not consider them to be full citizens of the Republic.[41]

What defines Tuareg above all is their mobility. They moved back and forth across the Sahara Desert, running caravans, controlling oases and junctures of trade routes, and establishing clan alliances and at times kingdoms that provided (at a price) protection for trans-Saharan travel and commerce. Neither the French nor the Malian government quite knew what to make of them, for their self-definition as much as mode of existence did not fit within territorial markers. But the ironic consequence of the generalization of the nation-state system around the world in the 1960s was that Tuareg grievances and aspirations came to be expressed in a form inconsistent with their history—a demand for a separate, territorially defined state to be carved out of the northern part of the Republic of Mali, to be named Azawad. Some Tuareg organized themselves into guerilla units—drawing on their experience of desert fighting—and armed conflict erupted periodically. The conflict took a turn for the worse in 2011, as many Tuareg who had served Libya's Mouamar Qadaffi as mercenaries returned to Mali after the dictator's fall—with their weapons. The Malian military officers who staged the coup of March 2012 justified their action by the ineffectiveness of government support of the army in its conflict with Tuareg militias. The effect of their action, however, was to accentuate the decomposition of the Malian army.

Another element of the conflict also fits uneasily with the post-1960 state system. An offshoot of the international *jihadist* network, Al Qaeda in the Islamic Maghreb (AQMI), established bases in the poorly controlled border region connecting Algeria and Mali, spilling into the desert regions of neighboring countries. AQMI stands for a universalistic vision of Islam, held above any other form of allegiance, and has had a certain—but up to now limited—appeal to young Muslims in Africa who have become relatively detached from their communities of origin and have little hope that the current local, national, regional, or global economy has anything to offer them. If news reports are to be believed, many of the fighters are not from the Mali region at all, but part of the *jihadist* diaspora, including many Arabs. But that is only one dimension of the Saharan situation, for another—of long standing—is traffics of various sorts, most notably now in drugs. South American narcotics transit the Atlantic to the Gulf of Guinea and then go by land across the desert to North Africa and then across the Mediterranean to eager consumers in Europe. Add to that a business that has old roots but has recently been resurrected—kidnapping for ransom, of hapless European tourists but more often of aid workers. If the roots of this situation lie in the inability of states to offer a modicum of benefits and security for all citizens, the development of armed networks renders states even more vulnerable. Tuareg militias for a time allied with AQMI and took over much of the country, threatening even the capital. But the Tuareg were outflanked by AQMI, which tried to impose its will—and its version of Islamic law—on countryside and town. According to some reports, the Islamists' harsh regulation of social life—especially in regard to women— were much resented, but they did assure the food supply and provide a minimum of social services in the towns, offering an alternative to a government capable of providing neither services nor justice.[42]

The crisis in Mali attracted the attention of ECOWAS, the Economic Community of West African States, the institutional framework for cooperation among West African governments, but it was unable to intervene militarily. Alarmed at the possibility of an Islamist state in West Africa, France took upon itself (officially at the request of the Mali government) the right to intervene and chased AQMI fighters out of the major Malian towns and into the Saharan hills.

As of this writing, the future of Mali is highly uncertain. Elections have been held, and civilian rule in Mali may or may not become a durable reality; compromise between the state and Tuareg groups (themselves disunited, as they long have been) may or may not be worked out. At least some of the Tuareg involved in the conflict see creating yet another nationstate as the answer to their grievances.

The debacle of the Republic of Mali recalls the goals of the Mali Federation: to avoid the zero-sum game of competition for control of the nation-state by diffusing sovereignty over different layers, to adapt the organization of government to the diverse patterns of local residence and mobility that corresponded to the actual history and social patterns of West Africa, to seek—and to construct—a broad sense of identification among Africans who shared certain elements of cultural life and a common experience of working within French institutions. Utopian? Perhaps. But the dystopia of northern Mali, or the Ivorian civil war of 2010–11, or the long history of authoritarian rule in Guinea remind us that what seems like the straightest path does not necessarily lead to a livable future.

Senghor and most other politicians in French West Africa between 1945 and 1960 were not arguing against "the state." Quite the contrary, they all saw the state as a key agent of forging a collective vision as well as of building the schools, roads, hospitals, and other facilities needed for a decent life and possibilities of progress in the twentieth century. Nor were they all critics of the idea of "nation," for they believed in building an ideological edifice in which their fellow citizens would participate, although they differed on the extent to which such a nation would be "Negro-African," in Senghor's formulation, or "Ivorian" within a multinational federation, in Houphouët-Boigny's sense of things.[43] They rarely (and only negatively) used the term nation-state, but the danger they feared can be seen in the hyphen between nation and state: the notion that a singular people should correspond to a single government. Such a structure turned the question of whose state it was—and who should be excluded from it—into a contest with high stakes. Hence the struggles in recent years over "ivoirité" or "Azawad."[44] Senghor, for one, foresaw the danger of dividing Africa into rigidly defined, resource-poor states. As president of an African nation-state, he could not—or at least did not—avoid it.

Conclusion

Africa in the World, Past, Present, Future

When we make "Africa"—or "Senegal" or "Ghana"—the focus of our thinking about the actions of government or the possibilities of economic development, we take for granted that these are the necessary and proper units of analysis. Yet we are talking about categories whose very existence in human imagination is a product of history, indeed a history of connections across large spaces. It is not a history of particular regions following their unique vocations nor is it a history of interaction of political units equivalent to each other in form, military or economic power, or self-conception. To find some characteristic of Africa that explains why so many of its people are poor or so many of its governments corrupt takes us out of history and proposes as explanations that which needs to be explained.

We do not need to oppose claims that Europe is rich because it has better institutions than anyone else with a vision of African innocence destroyed by vicious intrusions from outside. People from the African continent were both victims of the slave trade and colonial economies and actors in them, but participation was not symmetrical in structure or effects. It is those effects—not the assigning of primordial guilt to an ethnically or continentally defined category of humans—that concern us. Seeing Africa in the world, as Du Bois proposed in 1946, is not a matter of juxtaposing a neatly bounded Africa and a neatly bounded Europe but of examining how the world in which both regions came to be defined was produced, via the uneven, power-laden forms of connection. Africa's economic present is a co-creation, emerging out of long-term interactions among nonequivalent political and economic structures.

It is striking how recent was the creation of some of the units that now appear as the basic and inevitable components of the world. Most of the states that exist today are creations of the past sixty years. The world in 1945 was still a world of empires—in the immediate aftermath of the defeat of two of the most aggressive in recent history—and nation-states existed among colonies, protectorates, mandated territories, dominions, federations, and national republics. The route *out* of empire did not necessarily, as far as anybody at the time knew, lead to the independent, sovereign, territorial nation-state.

In the debate in French West Africa over whether empire could be transformed into something less hierarchical and more associative, we see the complexity of defining what a relevant political unit is. Empire citizenship was a particularly powerful notion, for it set the terms for making claims on resources, not on the basis of a putative linguistic or cultural commonality, but on the basis of historical connection—indeed a history that included conquest, exploitation, and discrimination. Thinking about the implications of claim-making in such a context puts a number of present-day issues in a certain perspective. A "we versus they" version of history—emphasizing comparison over connection—does not get us to an understanding of how the units we compare were constituted and how they shaped each other. It is not obvious either that a "we versus they" approach will help us think productively about the future.

Take, first of all, the question of foreign aid. Aid is aid and it is foreign because it crosses boundaries of sovereignty. When, in 1955, people living in the territory of Senegal sought better health facilities and schools and labor conditions equivalent to those of France, they were posing a demand as French citizens. They had representatives—albeit few—in the French legislature. In 1965, they were posing such demands as citizens of Senegal, a poor country whose major source of foreign exchange and government revenue was, literally, peanuts. They could ask for foreign aid but had no say in its distribution.

Even then the distinction between development at "home" and "overseas" was not perfectly sharp. What in France has been known since the 1960s as "amémagement du territoire" is in fact a development program for relatively poor regions of France whose central ideas and even some of the personnel responsible for implementing it were imported from French Africa after decolonization.[1] Foreign aid and regional development became separate programs in France, but their contents—the kind of projects proposed and the possibility of financing them from a larger, more inclusive unit—are similar.

The discourse around overseas development in French Africa before decolonization was about entitlements of citizens; after that it was about supplication. One of the main reasons why France moved away from centralizing strategies in 1956 was precisely to diminish the force of claims to entitlements from its neediest territories. Similarly, the British government, once it had hitched the legitimacy of its colonial empire to the notion of "development" in the 1940s, had to face the cost of meeting or resisting claims to higher wages and better social services made by people in the territories of Kenya, Nigeria, and so on based on their being "British." Once we see the change in sovereignty regimes as a recent and contingent process, not a long-term and inherent difference between "us" and "them," we might take a more supple view of what aid actually means.[2]

By pushing the "we" up to the level of the whole empire—a union of peoples rather than a people—both demanders and providers were thinking in ways that could point still further upward. Development discourse, so prevalent in the decades after World War II, suggested that there was a world level at which entitlements existed, that as citizens of the world people had minimal needs that their membership in a global community should entitle them to have met. The Universal Declaration of Human Rights of 1948 implied as much through its clauses on economic and social rights. But how does one construct a comprehensive health care system or an educational system accessible to all if one assumes that the resources available within a political unit should be the ones to define whether children should live or die, become literate or not?

To point to the contingency of the relationship of territorial state to human welfare not only opens the door to debate over the global distribution of resources, but renders problematic the argument made by rulers of some newly independent states that criticism of their actions from outside their borders constitutes interference—a form of neo-colonialism. To argue this way imputes sovereignty with a naturalness, permanence, and solidity that is inconsistent with the history of much of the world.

As recently as the late 1950s, political leaders in French Africa were appealing for a notion of sovereignty that was layered, that took into account both the particularity of territorial units and the usefulness and sense of shared history attached to a larger unit, acknowledging and moving beyond the violence and subordination that had created that unit.[3] Political activists in the post-World War II era were not just asserting the right to national self-determination, but also basic social and economic rights. French leaders, for a time, were eager enough to hold together the heterogeneous and unwieldy French Union that they engaged in give and take with African political movements over political and social issues despite their worries that implementing an empire of equal citizens would be extremely costly. The International Labor Organization became a forum for discussion of developing world-wide standards for labor conditions—a discussion that still goes on despite arguments from some powerful interests that labor issues are matters of national policy and by others that such matters should be left to "the market."[4] That national sovereignty should trump other rights was the outcome of political processes—and remains contested.[5]

Africans' claims on the French state are now distanced by the separation of sovereignties, but the history that shaped Africa and linked it to France and the rest of the world did not suddenly end in 1960. Breaking into the actually existing structures of national politics, international institutions, and corporate interests to suggest alternatives poses serious challenges of a practical and theoretical nature, but it might help to begin by discarding the assumption that the present-day order is either natural or inevitable.

The question of immigration might also be posed differently if one looks beyond the taken-for-granted quality of present borders. Before World War II, French Africans were not supposed to leave their own districts without permission of a local official, although many did. Between 1946 and 1960, they had the right as French citizens to circulate anywhere in the empire. Many could not afford the costs of migration, but they had the legal right to travel or move to any part of the French Union/Community and thousands sought jobs in metropolitan France.[6] They could join trade unions and claim the same wages as anyone else in the place they worked. They could apply to institutions of higher education and civil service jobs anywhere. They could move back and forth. They often experienced discrimination and denigration, but their representatives had a platform in the French legislature and a basis in the French elite's desire to hold some form of French community together to protest in the name of the equality of all French citizens.[7]

Although the citizenship concept did not have the same weight in the British Empire, the Nationality Act of 1948 posited a similar right of movement within the Empire. It was passed by Parliament in response to the attempts of Dominions to define their own citizenships and with the memory of the Empire's contribution to the war effort very much in mind, and it in effect created a second-tier status of "citizen of the United Kingdom and Colonies," derivative of Canadian, Australian, or other citizenship in a Commonwealth state, and it applied to colonial subjects as well. Although sentiment in the British Isles over the arrival of black migrants was mitigated, the logic of empire trumped the logic of race and Jamaicans or Nigerians had the legal right to enter.[8]

The change in sovereignty regime did not immediately end such connections. In negotiations over independence, French officials were so anxious that their own citizens could continue to go to and do business in newly independent African countries that they were willing to concede Africans the right to circulate freely in the newly defined nation-state of France. For a time, Africans born before independence had via bilateral treaties negotiated in 1960 some of the rights they had had as citizens of France before that date, and if they established residency in France they needed only to have their French nationality "recognized" if they so desired. They did not need to *become* French nationals. Such arrangements were made more palatable by the acute need France had for workers during the "trente glorieueses," the thirty years of economic growth after the war.

All that changed in the mid-1970s, as the French economy declined and "français de souche"—"true" French people—increasingly complained about people from North or sub-Saharan Africa taking up jobs they wanted. A law of 1974 all but eliminated work immigration. In Great Britain, prejudice and concerns with employment had been nibbling away at the rights of former subjects of empire to enter the country, and it was also in the 1970s that they were sharply restricted.[9]

The circuits of West Africans shifted from an intra-empire pattern, shaped by the regime of free circulation within the French Union and employers' interest in hiring people from categories with which they were familiar, to a highly restricted one. Having "papers" is crucial to one's life chances. So what distinguishes an immigrant from a citizen is not an essential quality of the person or even of the territory he or she is from; "immigrant" is a political construct and it has been and is subject to political and social reconstruction. One of the main complaints of the "sans-papiers" (undocumented) in France today is that their ancestors have been French citizens and have served France in war and peace; they claim that their history gives them certain entitlements. French governments and much of the populace do not see history that way. They have a point; independence matters. But the idea that the father was a citizen and the son a sans-papier is a basic source of the tension in today's France.[10]

Lest the "national" order of things seem entrenched in our present even if it was a less certain element of our past, one should consider the making of Europe in the context of the ending of empire. Even as alternatives for transforming empire into a federal or confederal structure were being discussed among African and French leaders after World War II, the possibility of a European political and economic community was also surfacing. The question was posed in the late 1940s of whether a continentally defined France or else a transcontinental, imperial France would participate. French and African leaders employed the term "Eurafrique"—previously a synonym for a European claim to African resources—to express the idea of folding Africa into the new project for a European community. As plans for a European economic or political community were discussed in the early 1950s, French leaders realized that joining Europe without Africa meant splitting the French Union. But Senghor and other African leaders insisted that if France were to join some kind of European confederation, they expected to have a full voice in its affairs. As Senghor put it in 1953, Africa did not want to be the dowry France paid to Germany as part of the marriage contract of the two former enemies.[11]

The issue came up in other discussions of possible forms of European cooperation. In internal discussions in 1956 over a shared European project on atomic energy, for example, French officials both pointed to the importance for all of Europe of African resources in uranium and to the fact that, as one put it, "the effort to develop African territories requires a gigantic effort that goes beyond our own means."[12]

We know the outcome: Eurafrique did not come into being—in no small part because other European states did not want to take on the burdens of empire—and the attempt to forge a Franco-African community foundered on conflict over how it should be constituted.[13] But France decided it wanted confederation for itself, ceding over time sovereign powers to a European entity it helped to construct. Former French African states were initially given the status of "associates" of the European Economic Community, but that status gave them no voice in its institutions. African territories were increasingly demarcated as "other." Later, open borders within Europe went along with an immigration wall around Europe, and some of Europe's others now risk their lives to cross the straits of Gibraltar or to get to the Canary Islands or to Sicily to sneak past the barrier.

The 1950s were ambiguous times, with methods of colonial control in ill-defined relationship to fledgling democratic institutions. We can point to heavy-handed French repression of a movement that had crossed an ill-defined line in Cameroon or trickery in electoral politics in Niger in 1958, but also to the presence of Africans—who could bring scandals to the public—in French legislative bodies and in assemblies that after 1957 exercised real power within each territory. The fact of regular, scheduled elections and the continued existence of parliamentary bodies meant that institutions for citizen participation in politics had been put in place—at quite a late date in the history of French colonization. African movements after 1945 focused on these institutions, even if there were a variety of relationships—personal, religious, ethnic—and a variety of discourses in different African idioms that also constituted politics. We see here the interplay of a variant of Senghor's idea of horizontal solidarity—a "people" working together through common institutions—with vertical connections—the systems of patronage and power that existed between French administrators and African elites, between party leaders in Africa and local political organizations and religious leaders, clan elders, chiefs, and so on. What made politics in the 1950s so volatile was the coexistence of horizontal and vertical connections.

It might be supposed that the end of colonialism constituted the triumph of horizontal solidarity—among Africans—over vertical. Yet within the independent nation-state, it became possible for each leader to dismantle citizenship structures that checked his exercise of vertical authority—hence the histories of moves toward authoritarian politics in Guinea, Côte d'Ivoire, and Senegal. Independence in the form of territorial nation-states meant that the overarching institutions, such as African participation in legislative bodies in French West Africa as a whole and in France, were eliminated, quite abruptly in the case of the Mali Federation.

Such institutions had represented a collective check, both Franco-African and Afro-African, on the actions of individual leaders in each territory. Relations among African states were quickly subordinated to the quest for power within each national unit.

But one should not assume that African states have become entirely detached from "society" or that the citizenship relationship that connected and challenged the relationship of state and society during decolonization cannot be revived. In an intriguing study conducted in the late 1990s, Lauren MacLean found quite different forms of social relationships in villages located on either side of the Ghana-Côte d'Ivoire border even though the villages were nearby and part of the same Akan ethnic complex. The political mobilization in the French territory around the concept of citizenship in the 1950s had long-term effects on people's expectations of the role of the state in their lives. MacLean found that villagers on the Côte d'Ivoire side of the border had a more "individualized, entitlement-based sense of citizenship" and greater focus on the nuclear family than their Ghanaian cousins, whose British pedigree did not include such a strong notion of citizenship and where the independent state since the 1960s had been failing to provide much of anything in the way of social services to its citizens. Ghanaian villages, in response, developed wider networks of cooperation among themselves. Social norms, MacLean is suggesting, are not independent of state policies. The relatively strong development of citizenship notions in Côte d'Ivoire—and the ability of the state to make at least partly good on its end of the citizen-state bargain until its crisis of the 1990s—were inscribed in village-level, family-level social relations.[14]

This local study underscores the long-term importance of a development than can be observed at a higher level of generality. In many African countries, people did get something from their citizenship during the first decade and a half of the era of independence: educational access shot upward, including at secondary and tertiary levels, literacy became more widespread, infant mortality declined, and life expectancy rose. The standard measures of economic growth fluctuated from place to place and time to time, but until the mid-1970s they were on the whole mildly positive. This was a period when most governments, including some run by authoritarian rulers, believed that, however much they directed resources to themselves and their clients, they had to deliver at least something to their citizens—education, health services, roads. What they could not do—hardly surprising in the historical context described in these pages—

was oversee the improvement of well-being sufficiently broad and deep to
contain tensions over who was getting those resources or build "national"
economies capable of withstanding the vagaries of world markets. The
inability to achieve these ends conditioned governments' widespread tendency to repress opposition—whose demands could not be met—and to
engage in a politics of patronage for the supporters on whom they depended.
The world recession of the 1970s turned modest possibilities into economic catastrophe over much of the continent, and the policies of international financial agencies—above all the insistence on balancing budgets
and cutting whatever social services existed—made long-term recovery
even more difficult. However critical one can be of African states' conduct
of economic affairs in the 1960s, the more "market" oriented policies
imposed by international financial organizations—and a host of
"experts"—in the late 1970s produced results between the mitigated and
the disastrous.[15]

We should neither exaggerate what states accomplished with their independence in the first decade nor assimilate the malaise of the last decades
to a general African condition. We need instead to look beyond states and
societies as abstractions and examine with a finer lens what states did and
can do—and what cannot be done without them—in the context of a
varied and complex continent and a world economy that remains highly
unequal.

The intertwining of Africa, Europe, and the Americas has another
dimension. The diminished capacity of African states, especially after the
1970s, to administer effective bureaucracies and legal systems makes them
porous to all sorts of international traffics—arms, drugs, dubious land
deals, dumping of waste products, and so on. As Stephen Ellis puts it, a
state "can rent out its sovereign rights for quite small amounts of cash and
can offer important facilities for professional law-breakers of every sort."[16]
It takes two sides for such processes to take place—elements within a
government or in some cases regional warlords and elements from outside
who have something to offer and to gain. The condition that makes such
connections likely to be made is the extreme asymmetry in global economic relations. This condition has a long history. A government that is
responsible to its people, with a press free to disclose scandals, and—
above all—capable of offering regular and predictable services through
official channels to its citizens is perhaps the most likely antidote to such
dubious linkages. The outside world has not necessarily helped bring

about such possibilities. The undermining of state capacities during the era of structural adjustment made a difficult situation worse. It is far from clear that the damage can be undone with the resources that many African states currently possess. At present, however, there a few hopeful signs in some countries—Ghana for instance—that state capacity to raise money in open capital markets and deliver at least some services is increasing and that public discourse about these subjects constrains illicit economic networks.

In Africa, citizen mobilization has often been repressed, but it also reappears. Take the 2012 election in Senegal. When the incumbent Abdoulaye Wade (who had himself defeated the incumbent Abdou Diouf in 2000) tried to facilitate his reelection by changing rules of the electoral system, people, especially young people in Dakar, took to the streets. Rap musicians were among those who contributed to a public mobilization for a fair election. The government backed off its attempt to change the rules, and rather to the surprise of many Senegalese intellectuals, the election turned out to be reasonably fair. It resulted, for the second time in recent Senegalese history, in a sitting president accepting defeat. Since the 1990s, when a combination of external and internal pressures pushed many African governments to allow multiple parties and elections, some political openings have been manipulated from above but others have brought citizens together to bring about a change of government.[17]

African states do not make history as they might wish. They exist in the world. Not surprisingly, the rulers of many African states have seen less advantage in cooperating with each other—Senghor's horizontal solidarity—than in cultivating vertical relationships with richer states. France has not disappeared from the West African scene, but the structure of relationships changed. Decolonization took those relationships out of the relatively open institutions—legislatures and councils—in which leaders from both sides had participated since 1946, however unequally, and put them into two categories: formal, diplomatic relations between states and back-office relationships. Henceforth, Jacques Foccart, the French President's "Monsieur Afrique" operating out of the Elysée Palace, was able to construct his network of patron-client relations with African leaders, one by one.[18] We see here the transition from a structure of layered politics that combined horizontal and vertical elements—in which inequality was frankly admitted and made into an explicit object of reform—to one that was formally that of equivalent nation-states, but whose reality was highly skewed, unchecked by citizenship structures above those of the nation-state itself.

Taken together, sovereignty and clientage bring resources to governing elites. Whether such resources benefit most of the people in African countries is another question. The quest for a patron appears to many a more realistic way to betterment than the mobilization of a citizenry. On the international level, a rich country—or indeed a transnational corporation—is free to pick and choose which leaders it wants to deal with, whom it wants to aid, what parts of Africa are interesting economically. We are back, in effect, to a notion advocated by some French colonial interests in the 1930s (Chapter 1) of focusing on a "useful Africa," those parts of Africa with oil, uranium, or cocoa, or which present a strategic interest (or a strategic danger), while leaving the rest to its fate.

Senghor's argument for combining vertical and horizontal relationships acknowledged the reality colonization had accentuated—the asymmetry of the relationship of any African territory with the wealthy countries of Europe and North America (and one can now add East Asia). It was a reality that after independence could be hidden behind a facade of sovereign equality. European countries could choose to compromise their sovereignty to constitute the European Economic Community and then the European Union, but the sovereignty of African states was far more fragile. Decolonization in itself did not have to make it so, but the particular process of decolonization that Africa experienced—what Senghor called balkanization—made sovereignty the principle asset that governing elites had to deploy. There are occasional signs of renewed African interest in cross-state cooperation, even if the African Union remains largely a mutual protection society of heads of state. The southern and western African regional organizations (SADCC and ECOWAS) point in a direction of cooperation—but their willingness and ability to act has been quite uneven, especially when it came to issues of human rights in African regimes. Yet the ups and downs of electoral politics in different countries remind us that historical trends do not all go in one direction.

My goal in these pages has not been to prescribe specific measures for rich nations and international organizations to reconfigure trade, finance, and aid or to tell African governments what their economic and social policies should be. It has been instead to pull back a step and to suggest the need to rethink the way in which we frame such considerations, looking beyond the false dichotomies of "Africa" and "the world economy," of "market" and "state," of "aid" and "local development," of the "sovereign state" and "foreign interference." All these concepts are the products of history, in some respects going back to the era of the slave trade, in some respects as recent as the last half-century. Their present meanings may not prove durable, and "global" institutions should be subject to reexamination as much as are the behaviors and policies of African states.

Alternative pathways were opened up at different moments of African history, not least in the critical and uncertain decades in which a future beyond colonial empire was in question. The patterns we often see as built into global structures do not necessarily have the solidity we think they possess. They were born of contingent and contested political processes, which we might not notice if we do our history backward, assuming that the path to our present was the only option in the past. The possibilities for the future are not same as those that were open when Du Bois published his *The World and Africa* in 1946, but we need to remember that they are multiple.

Notes

Introduction

1. W. E. B. Du Bois, *The World and Africa: An Inquiry into the Part which Africa Has Played in World History* (New York: International Publishers, 1965, originally published by Viking in 1946). Du Bois pointed out in his preface to the 1946 edition that he was providing an enlarged and revised version of his 1939 book *Black Folk: Then and Now*. The earlier book had been written at the end of an age of European dominance, but the new version was appearing "at the threshold of a change of which I had not dreamed in 1935." His goal now was "not so much a history of the Negroid peoples as a statement of their integral role in human history from prehistoric to modern times." "Foreword," viii.

2. The impact of these events on British thinking about labor and economic development is discussed in Frederick Cooper, *Decolonization and African Society: The Labor Question in French and British Africa* (Cambridge: Cambridge University Press, 1996), Chapter 3.

3. Penny M. von Eschen, *Race against Empire: Black Americans and Anticolonialism, 1937–1957* (Ithaca: Cornell University Press, 1997). The phrase quoted comes from a letter of the Community Progressive Negro Painters Union and the New Harlem Tenants League to the Mayor of New York, May 15, 1946, cited in ibid., 69. Von Eschen argues that this moment was a high point of African American involvement in African liberation, for in the ensuing years both the gains that appeared possible through a domestically focused campaign for civil rights and the dangers of repression

for taking liberation too far in the context of the Cold War led to an inward turn by the most influential organizations of African Americans.

4. C. L. R. James, *The Black Jacobins: Toussaint L'Ouverture and the San Domingo Revolution* (New York: Dial Press, 1938). The book has since been republished in a number of editions. Another West Indian who saw the strike wave as a sign of crisis in the empire was W. Arthur Lewis, then a graduate student in London and a future winner of the Nobel Prize in economics. See his pamphlet *Labour in the West Indies* (London: Fabian Society, 1939).

5. Michel-Rolph Trouillot, *Silencing the Past: Power and the Production of History* (Boston: Beacon, 1995). On the sugar plantation as part of an emerging transatlantic capitalist system, see also Sidney Mintz, *Sweetness and Power: The Place of Sugar in Modern History* (New York: Penguin, 1985).

6. The Haitian revolution did not get the attention it deserved for many years after James's book but has by now become a major focus of scholarly attention. See for example Carolyn Fick, *The Making of Haiti: The Saint Domingue Revolution from Below* (Knoxville: University of Tennessee Press, 1990); Laurent Dubois, *Avengers of the New World: The Story of the Haitian Revolution* (Cambridge, MA: Harvard University Press, 2004); Jeremy Popkin, *A Concise History of the Haitian Revolution* (Malden, MA: Wiley-Blackwell, 2012).

7. Eric Williams, *Capitalism and Slavery* (Chapel Hill: University of North Carolina Press, 1944). See the biography by Colin Palmer, *Eric Williams & the Making of the Modern Caribbean* (Chapel Hill: University of North Carolina Press, 2006).

8. Melville Herskovits, "Native Self-Government," *Foreign Affairs* 22 (1944): 413–23. For the request for responses to Herskovits's article, see Commissaire aux Colonies to Governor General, Afrique Occidentale Française, August 5, 1944, 17G 133, Archives of Senegal. This dossier also contains the responses. Herskovits had, before the war, studied populations of African origin in the Americas as well as in Africa, and he was exploring the connections between the two, notably in *The Myth of the Negro Past* (New York: Harper, 1941). His evocations of African models for future governments emerged from his field research in West Africa, *Dahomey, an Ancient African Kingdom* (New York: Augustin, 1938).

9. Robert Lemaignen, Léopold Sédar Senghor, and Prince Sisonath Youtévong, *La communauté impériale française* (Paris: Alsatia, 1945). Senghor's chapter appears on pp. 57–98. The debates on restructuring the French empire after the war will be discussed in Chapter 3.

10. Aimé Césaire, *Discours sur le colonialisme* (Paris: Réclame, 1950). This short book went through several French editions and was later translated into English by Joan Pinkham as *Discourse on Colonialism* (New York: Monthly Review Press, 1972). On the international dimensions of some of this literature, see Brent Hayes Edwards, *The Practice of Diaspora: Literature, Translation, and the Rise of Black Internationalism* (Cambridge: Harvard University Press, 2003).

11. John Lonsdale, "States and Social Processes in Africa: A Historiographical Survey," *African Studies Review* 24, no. 2/3 (1981): 139–225, 143 quoted. My own contribution to the same journal began my thinking about some of the issues discussed in the following pages. "Africa and the World Economy," ibid., 1–86.

12. The earlier "Congo Crisis" (beginning in 1960) was certainly a warning that independence might not be the end-point Africans and empathetic foreigners hoped for, but it could be attributed to the incompetent way in which Belgium prepared for the handover and the machinations of foreign powers. The coup against Nkrumah, who had been head of state of Ghana for nine years and in charge of internal affairs of that territory for fifteen, was more disillusioning. For a gripping fictional account of disillusionment with the post-independent state, see Ayi Kwei Armah, *The Beautyful Ones Are Not Yet Born* (London: Heinemann, 1968).

1. Africa and Capitalism

1. For a classic example, see David Landes, *The Wealth and Poverty of Nations: Why Some Are So Rich and Some So Poor* (New York: Norton, 1998). A more recent and more subtle comparative argument is Daron Acemoglu and James Robinson, *Why Nations Fail: The Origins of Power, Prosperity and Poverty* (New York: Crown Publishers, 2012).

2. Kenneth Pomeranz, *The Great Divergence: China, Europe, and the Making of the Modern World Economy* (Princeton: Princeton University Press, 2000); Prasannan Parthasarathi, *Why Europe Grew Rich and Asia Did Not: Global Economic Divergence, 1600–1850* (Cambridge: Cambridge University Press, 2011). Since the publication of Pomeranz's book, many scholars have both taken issue with some of its arguments and tried to build on his insights. See for example the forum on "Asia and Europe in the World Economy," in *American Historical Review* 107, no. 2 (2002): 419–80, including contributions of Pomeranz, R. Bin Wong, Patrick Manning, and David Ludden. See also the review by Jan de Vries of Parthasarathi's book in ibid., 117 (2012): 1532–34.

3. Pomeranz, 11. The other principle factor, according to Pomeranz, that made steam-powered industrial machinery especially attractive in England was the availability of coal. The importance of sugar in providing the caloric basis for an industrial labor force was earlier emphasized by Sidney Mintz, *Sweetness and Power: The Place of Sugar in Modern History* (New York: Penguin, 1985).

4 John Brewer, *The Sinews of Power: War, Money, and the English State, 1688–1783* (New York: Knopf, 1989).

5. Among a large literature on industrialization in Asia and other "late" developers, see Alice Amsden, *The Rise of "The Rest": Challenges to the West from Late-Industrializing Economies* (Oxford: Oxford University Press, 2001).

6. For an interpretation of the longue durée of African history that puts considerable weight on questions of population, see John Iliffe, *Africans: The History of a*

Continent, 2nd ed. (Cambridge: Cambridge University Press, 2007). Iliffe does not posit a mechanical relationship between population density and certain political forms, but rather analyzes different political and social adaptations to differential population density.

7. The complexities of land tenure in pre-conquest Africa and the effects of colonization on land rights and access are beginning to get the attention they deserve. See for example R. Kuba and Carola Lentz, eds., *Land and the Politics of Belonging in West Africa* (Leiden: Brill, 2006). On the complex ways of understanding wealth in people, see the pioneering work of Jane I. Guyer and Samuel M. Eno Belinga, "Wealth in People as Wealth in Knowledge: Accumulation and Composition in Equatorial Africa," *The Journal of African History* 36 (1995): 91–120.

8. The literature on slavery in Africa has grown from practically nothing in the early 1970s to a large and still-growing field. For a summary, see Paul Lovejoy, *Transformations in Slavery: A History of Slavery in Africa,* 3rd ed. (Cambridge: Cambridge University Press, 2012). My earliest research in African history was on this subject: *Plantation Slavery on the East Coast of Africa in the Nineteenth Century* (New Haven: Yale University Press, 1977) and "The Problem of Slavery in African Studies," *Journal of African History* 20 (1979): 103–25.

9. Albert Hirschman, *Exit, Voice, and Loyalty: Responses to Decline in Firms, Organizations, and States* (Cambridge, MA: Harvard University Press, 1970).

10. Ghislaine Lydon, *On Trans-Saharan Trails: Islamic Law, Trade Networks, and Cross-cultural Exchange in Nineteenth-century Western Africa* (Cambridge: Cambridge University Press, 2009).

11. Toby Green, *The Rise of the Trans-Altantic Slave Trade in Western Africa, 1800–1589* (Cambridge: Cambridge University Press, 2012).

12. Linda Newson, "Africans and Luso-Africans in the Portuguese Slave Trade of the Upper Guinea Coast in the Early Seventeenth Century," *Journal of African History* 53 (2012): 1–24. On the importance of Luso-Africans to the Angola slave trade, see Joseph Miller, *Way of Death: Merchant Capitalism and the Angolan Slave Trade, 1730–1830* (Madison: University of Wisconsin Press, 1988), 245–83.

13. G. Ugo Nwokeji, *The Slave Trade and Culture in the Bight of Biafra: An African Society in the Atlantic World* (Cambridge: Cambridge University Press, 2010); Linda Heywood and John Thornton, *Central Africans, Atlantic Creoles, and the Foundation of the Americas, 1585–1660* (Cambridge: Cambridge University Press, 2007). The word "creole" may smooth out such processes too much, as well as assume more coherence to the prior social arrangements that each "side" brought to the encounter. In a sense all societies are creolized, but not in the same way or the same degree and not necessarily acknowledging their mixity. The point to emphasize is the interface between different social and economic networks, producing a variety of social formations, sometimes giving rise to sexual and cultural mixtures, sometimes to uneasy juxtapositions

of collectivities doing business with each other, sometimes to volatile military alliances and conflicts.

14. Jane Guyer, "Introduction: The Currency Interface and Its Dynamics," in Jane Guyer, ed., *Money Matters: Instability, Values and Social Payments in the Modern History of West African Communities* (Portsmouth: Heinemann, 1995), 7–8.

15. Some of the biggest kingdoms in West Africa obtained many of their export slaves by purchase, deriving their income from acting as middlemen. Robin Law, *The Oyo Empire, c.1600–c.1836: A West African Imperialism in the Era of the Atlantic Slave Trade* (Oxford: Clarendon Press, 1977), 306.

16. The literature on the slave trade is by now immense. For pioneering work, see Walter Rodney, *A History of the Upper Guinea Coast, 1545–1800* (Oxford: Clarendon, 1970); Walter Rodney, *How Europe Underdeveloped Africa* (London: Bogle-L'Ouverture, 1972); and Philip Curtin, *The African Slave Trade: A Census* (Madison: University of Wisconsin Press, 1969). Estimates of the numbers involved have continuously been revised. Curtin powerfully debunked some of the earlier estimates—of the order of twenty million people sent across the Atlantic between the fifteenth and nineteenth centuries—pointing out that they were based on little actual quantitative evidence. His estimates—around nine million—based largely on records of slave traders have been revised upward as new sources were uncovered and quantitative methods became more sophisticated. David Eltis and David Richardson, *Atlas of the Transatlantic Slave Trade* (New Haven: Yale University Press, 2010); David Eltis, Stephen Behrendt, David Richardson, and Herbert Klein, *The Trans-atlantic Slave Trade: A Database on CD-ROM* (Cambridge: Cambridge University Press, 1999). Another series of works focuses on the polities that were most active in the slave trade. In addition to work already cited, see Kristin Mann, *Slavery and the Birth of an African City: Lagos, 1760–1900* (Bloomington: Indiana University Press, 2007); Boubacar Barry, *Senegambia and the Atlantic Slave Trade,* trans. Ayi Kwei Armah (Cambridge: Cambridge University Press, 1998), and James Searing, *West African Slavery and Atlantic Commerce the Senegal River Valley, 1700–1860* (Cambridge: Cambridge University Press, 1993). General studies include Patrick Manning, *Slavery and African life: Occidental, Oriental, and African Slave Trades* (Cambridge: Cambridge University Press, 1990); John Thornton, *Africa and Africans in the Making of the Atlantic World, 1400–1800* (Cambridge: Cambridge University Press, 1998); J. E. Inikori, *Africans and the Industrial Revolution in England: A Study in International Trade and Development* (Cambridge: Cambridge University Press, 2002).

17. James McCann, "Maize and Grace: History, Corn, and Africa's New Landscapes, 1500–1999," *Comparative Studies in Society and History* 43 (2001); 246–72, esp. 258.

18. Miller's long study of the Angola slave trade concludes that it "linked the two conceptually opposed and spatially separated but complementary forms of political economy, those in Africa and the one from beyond the Atlantic." *Way of Death,* 674.

19. For a time, historians debated whether most slaves were the by-products of wars waged for political reasons or whether the overseas market in slaves stimulated raiding. The best answer is a dialectical one: the overseas outlet changed the nature of politics and war.

20. The pioneering work on the "reproduction" of slave populations through continued importation—as second-generation slaves moved into a less demeaning, alienable, and exploitable status—appeared in Claude Meillassoux, ed., *L'Esclavage en Afrique précoloniale* (Paris: Maspero, 1975), and the same author's *Anthropologie de l'esclavage: le ventre de fer et d'argent* (Paris: Presses Universitaires de France, 1986). On the nineteenth-century expansion of slave-based agriculture, see Lovejoy, *Transformations in Slavery,* as well as numerous case studies, including my own *Plantation Slavery.*

21. Karl Marx, *Capital: Volume One,* trans. Ben Fowkes (New York: Vintage, 1977). There have been a host of interpretations taking off from Marx. Two influential ones are Robert Brenner, "The Origins of Capitalist Development: A Critique of neo-Smithian Marxism," *New Left Review* 104 (1977): 25–92, and Richard Biernacki, *The Fabrication of Labor: Germany and Britain, 1640–1914* (Berkeley: University of California Press, 1995).

22. This ambiguous realm—from the Master and Servant Ordinances that gave employers instruments to exercise power over workers in England until the twentieth century to forms of indentured labor that amounted to enslavement with an expiration date but were fetishized as a "contract" between worker and employer—have been receiving increased attention from historians lately. See for example Alessandro Stanziani. "Labour Institutions in a Global Perspective, from the Seventeenth to the Twentieth Century," *International Review of Social History* 54 (2009): 351–358, and "The Traveling Panopticon: Labor Institutions and Labor Practices in Russia and Britain in the Eighteenth and Nineteenth Centuries," *Comparative Studies in Society and History,* 51 (2009): 715–741.

23. Eric Williams had argued in *Capitalism and Slavery* that slavery was abolished in British colonies because it was no longer profitable, but there is evidence to the contrary, particularly the sugar boom in Spanish Cuba that took place after emancipation on the British West Indies. More persuasive is the argument of David Brion Davis that antislavery was an ideological concomitant of the development of capitalism. *The Problem of Slavery in the Age of Revolution 1770–1823* (Ithaca: Cornell University Press, 1975). Seymour Drescher has provided alternative analyses in a series of books, including *The Mighty Experiment: Free Labor Versus Slavery in British Emancipation* (Oxford: Oxford University Press, 2002).

24. Shlomo Avineri, ed., *Karl Marx on Colonialism and Modernization; His Despatches and Other Writings on China, India, Mexico, the Middle East and North Africa* (Garden City, NY: Doubleday, 1969).

25. A classic statement of such an argument is David Washbrook, "Law, State and Agrarian Society in Colonial India," *Modern Asian Studies* 15 (1981): 649–721. For a

more recent review, see Sabyasachi Bhattacharya, "Paradigms in the Historical Approach to Labour Studies on South Asia," in Jan Lucassen, ed., *Global Labour History: A State of the Art* (Bern: Peter Lang, 2006), and David Ludden, ed., *The New Cambridge History of India. IV.4, An Agrarian History of South Asia* (Cambridge: Cambridge University Press, 2008).

26. David Livingstone, *Missionary travels and researches in South Africa; including a sketch of sixteen years' residence in the interior of Africa, and a journey from the Cape of Good Hope to Loanda, on the west coast; thence across the continent, down the river Zambesi, to the eastern ocean* (London: Murray, 1857).

27. A cogent argument for the way British colonizers in Africa pulled their punches on the economic front comes from Anne Phillips, *The Enigma of Empire: British Policy in West Africa* (Bloomington: Indiana University Press, 1989). For a detailed case study of an attempt to turn slave labor into wage labor and the inability of the state to accomplish such a task in anything like the form initially sought, see my *From Slaves to Squatters: Plantation Labor and Agriculture in Zanzibar and Coastal Kenya, 1890–1925* (New Haven: Yale University Press, 1980).

28. Jean-François Bayart, "Africa in the World: a History of Extroversion," *African Affairs* 99 (1999): 217–26. For a related argument, see my "Africa and the World Economy," *African Studies Review* 24 (1981): 1–86.

29. Edmond Giscard d'Estaing, "Rapport de M. Giscard d'Estaing," April 18, 1932, AP 539/1, in Archives d'Outre-Mer, Aix-en-Provence, France.

30. Eric Allina, *Slavery by Any Other Name: African Life under Company Rule in Colonial Mozambique* (Charlottesville: University of Virginia Press, 2012).

31. Stanley Trapido, "Landlord and Tenant in a Colonial Economy: The Transvaal 1880–1900," *Journal of Southern African Studies* 5 (1978): 26–58.

32. How an African navigated these rough waters is poignantly described by Charles van Onselen, *The Seed Is Mine: The Life of Kas Maine, a South African Sharecropper, 1894–1985* (New York: Hill and Wang, 1996).

33. The limited extent of capital investment in African colonies has been known for some time. S. Herbert Frankel, *Capital Investment in Africa: Its Course and Effects* (Oxford: Oxford University Press, 1938). That public investment in French West Africa came mainly after World War II is pointed out by Elise Huillery, " 'The Black Man's Burden—The Cost of Colonization of French West Africa for French Taxpayers," Paris School of Economics Working Paper 2009–22, http://halshs.archives-ouvertes .fr/docs/00/56/76/62/PDF/wp200922.pdf, accessed June 25, 2013.

34. Sara Berry, *No Condition Is Permanent: The Social Dynamics of Agrarian Change in Sub-Saharan Africa* (Madison: University of Wisconsin Press, 1993); Gareth Austin, *Labour, Land, and Capital in Ghana: From Slavery to Free Labor in Asante, 1807–1956* (Rochester: Rochester University Press, 2004); Polly Hill, *The Migrant Cocoa-farmers of Southern Ghana; A Study in Rural Capitalism* (Cambridge: Cambridge University Press, 1963).

35. In the late 1930s, cocoa farmers challenged the European-based cocoa-buying firms by holding back their harvests. They succeeded in getting the government to intervene and set up an alternative marketing system, but the conflict brought out tension between large-scale planters and the less well off in the region.

36. Sara Berry, *Fathers Work for Their Sons: Accumulation, Mobility, and Class Formation in an Extended Yorùbá Community* (Berkeley: University of California Press, 1985).

37. The model of modest-scale agricultural entrepreneur applies to coffee production in the Mt. Kilimanjaro region of Tanzania and in parts of highland Kenya and to varying degrees to other regions of cash-crop production. One can distinguish variations on the theme: specific kinds of social relations are conducive to the mobilization of labor for new forms of agricultural production and export.

38. Governor General Bernard Cornut-Gentile, "Memoire sur l'exécution du plan d'équipement en Afrique Equatorial Française pendant les exercises 1947–48 et 1948–49" (Brazzaville: Imprimerie Officielle); M. Moreau to Conférence d'Etudes des Plans, 29 November 1950, Compte Rendu, Affaires Economiques 169; "Observations et conclusions personnelles du Gouverneur Roland Pré, Président de la Commission d'Etude et de Coordination des Plans de Modernisation et d'Equipement des Territoires d'Outre-Mer," May 1954, mimeograph, all in Archives d'Outre-Mer, Aix-en-Provence.

39. Secretary of State Arthur Creech Jones, Circular Letter, 22 February 1947, CO 852/1003/3, National Archives of the United Kingdom. More generally on this theme, see Frederick Cooper, "Modernizing Bureaucrats, Backward Africans, and the Development Concept," in Frederick Cooper and Randall Packard, eds., *International Development and the Social Sciences: Essays in the History and Politics of Knowledge* (Berkeley: University of California Press, 1997), 64–92.

40. For a well-documented narrative of British development policy, see Michael Havinden and David Meredith, *Colonialism and Development: Britain and Its Tropical Colonies, 1850–1960* (London: Routledge, 1993). Development history is becoming a lively subfield. See for example the articles collected in a special issue of *Journal of Modern European History*, 8, no. 1 (2010).

41. These paragraphs are based on an analysis developed at length in my *Decolonization and African Society: The Labor Question in French and British Africa* (Cambridge: Cambridge University Press, 1996).

42. The supposedly "modern" currency regime to which colonial regimes tied their colonies also tied them to the difficulties of the franc and sterling zones and represented a serious constraint on credit at a time when France and Britain were in principle trying to expand public and private investment. On currency issues in late colonial and post-colonial regimes—including the underexamined alternative of "informal" credit arrangement in African societies—see Guyer, "Currency Interface," esp. 17–18.

43. Steven Feierman, *Peasant Intellectuals: Anthropology and History in Tanzania* (Madison: University of Wisconsin Press, 1990).

44. Todd Shepard, *The Invention of Decolonization: The Algerian War and the Remaking of France* (Ithaca: Cornell University Press, 2006); David Anderson, *Histories of the Hanged: Britain's Dirty War and the End of Empire* (New York: Norton, 2005).

45. In France, the argument went public in 1956 with a much-cited article in a popular magazine making the conservative case for decolonization: the African colonies did not pay. The issue is discussed in Cooper, *Decolonization and African Society,* Chapter 10.

46. Deepek Lal, *The Poverty of Development Economics* (Cambridge, MA: Harvard University Press for the Institute of Economic Affairs, 1985).

47. Differing perspectives on development are discussed in the introduction and articles in Cooper and Packard, *International Development and the Social Sciences.*

48. A now-classic study of how development agencies often focused on a non-problem—an aboriginal state of poverty and non-market orientations—while being unable to analyze the on-the-ground structures of the economy is James Ferguson, *The Anti-politics Machine: "Development," Depoliticization, and Bureaucratic Power in Lesotho* (Cambridge: Cambridge University Press, 1990).

49. The concept of the gatekeeper state is developed in Frederick Cooper, *Africa since 1940: The Past of the Present* (Cambridge: Cambridge University Press, 2002). See also Jean-François Bayart, *The State in Africa,* 2nd ed. (Cambridge: Polity, 2009), and Paul Nugent, *Africa since Independence: A Comparative History* (New York: Palgrave Macmillan, 2012).

50. The consequence of such networks is often termed warlordism. As William Reno points out, warlords were often high officials who could not quite make it to the top, developed regional power bases, obtained access to arms, and set out to conquer the state of which they had been a part. If successful the warlord could then become the head of state. *Warfare in Independent Africa* (Cambridge: Cambridge University Press, 2011).

51. See for example M. Anne Pitcher, *Transforming Mozambique: The Politics of Privatization, 1975–2000* (Cambridge: Cambridge University Press, 2002).

52. Jeremy Seekings and Nicoli Nattrass, *Class, Race, and Inequality in South Africa* (New Haven: Yale University Press, 2005).

53. This influential argument was initially set out in Daron Acemoglu and James Robinson, "The Colonial Origins of Comparative Development: An Empirical Investigation," *American Economic Review* 91 (2001): 1366–1401, and generalized around the world in their *Why Nations Fail.* For a perceptive critique of the overall thesis, see Gareth Austin, "The 'Reversal of Fortune' Thesis and the Compression of History: Perspectives from African and Comparative Economic History," *Journal of International Development* 20 (2008): 996–1027.

54. This is an example of what I earlier called the fallacy of the leapfrogging legacy. Frederick Cooper, *Colonialism in Question: Theory, Knowledge, History* (Berkeley: University of California Press, 2005), 17–18.

55. Morten Jerven, "African Economic Growth Recurring: An Economic History Perspective on African Growth Episodes, 1690–2010," *Economic History of Developing Regions* 25 (2010): 127–54.

56. Elise Huillery, "History Matters: The Long-term Impact of Colonial Public Investments in French West Africa," *American Economic Journal—Applied Economics* 1 (2009): 176–215.

57. For a historian's balanced assessment of the era of structural adjustment, see Nugent, *Africa Since Independence,* 328–47, and for an anthropologist's view of the effect of such policies on an African society, see James Ferguson, *Expectations of Modernity: Myths and Meanings of Urban Life on the Zambian Copperbelt* (Berkeley: University of California Press, 1999). See also Thandika Mkandawire and Charles Soludo, *Our Continent, Our Future: African Perspectives on Structural Adjustment* (Dakar: CODESRIA, 1999), and Nicolas Van de Walle, *African Economies and the Politics of Permanent Crisis, 1979–99* (Cambridge: Cambridge University Press, 2001).

58. See for example an article of two World Bank economists who emphasize sustained growth since 2000, reduction in poverty rates, and evidence of improved macroeconomic policy but who remain skeptical about structural change. They see the best hope for Africa in the larger number of people who have been educated and in improved communications, particularly because of the cell phone, both giving rise to increased pressure on governments to act in the public interest. Shantayanan Devarajan and Wolfgang Fengler, "Africa's Economic Boom," *Foreign Affairs* 92, no. 3 (2013): 68–81.

59. Stephen Ellis, *Season of Rains: Africa in the World* (Chicago: University of Chicago Press, 2012), 28. On the important—and volatile—case of Zambian copper, see Miles Larmer, "Historical Perspectives on Zambia's Mining Booms and Busts," and Ching Kwan Lee, "Raw Encounters: Chinese Managers, African Workers, and the Politics of Casualization in Africa's Chinese Enclaves," both in Alastair Fraser and Miles Larmer, eds., *Zambia, Mining, and Neoliberalism: Boom and Bust on the Globalized Copperbelt* (Houndmills, UK: Palgrave Macmillan, 2010), 31–58, 127–54.

60. Jerven also warns about statistical artifacts. Ghana's official GDP increased 60 percent in one year—an impossibility in real terms. The methods of calculation had in fact changed, and while the current methods might be more accurate, the previous output was probably not as bad as statistics suggested—although it was bad enough. Morten Jerven, *Poor Numbers: How We Are Misled by African Development Statistics and What to Do about It* (Ithaca: Cornell University Press, 2013).

61. Elise Huillery, "Colonization, Institutions and Development in the Former French West Africa," http://www.csae.ox.ac.uk/conferences/2006-eoi-rpi/papers /csae/huillery.pdf, accessed June 4, 2013.

62. Of the many reflections on the inadequacy of the post-1970s economic ortho-
doxy in relation to Africa, see James Ferguson, *Global Shadows: Africa in the Neoliberal
World Order* (Durham: Duke University Press, 2006).

63. Lydia Polgreen, "In Niger, Trees and Crops Turn Back the Desert," *New York
Times,* February 11, 2007.

64. Michael Kugelman and Susan Levenstein, eds., *The Global Farms Race: Land
Grabs, Agricultural Investment and the Scramble for Food Security* (Washington: Island
Press, 2013); Pauline Peters, "Conflicts over Land and Threats to Customary Tenure in
Africa," *African Affairs* 112 (2013): 543–62. These interventions do not condemn all
land alienation but emphasize the skewed power relations they entail, lack of trans-
parency, and risks to African cultivators.

2. Africa and Empire

1. W. E. B. Du Bois, *The Souls of Black Folk* (Chicago: McClurg, 1903), 1.

2. On the concept of empire and the variety of its repertoires of rule, see Jane
Burbank and Frederick Cooper, *Empires in World History: Power and the Politics of
Difference* (Princeton: Princeton University Press, 2010).

3. Susan Keech McIntosh, "Pathways to Complexity: An African Perspective," in
McIntosh, ed., *Beyond Chiefdoms: Pathways to Complexity in Africa* (Cambridge:
Cambridge University Press, 1999), 1–30, 2 quoted.

4. Ghana was defeated by the Almoravids in 1076 but reconstituted itself in a more
Islamic guise. For an introduction, see Nehemia Levtzion, *Ancient Ghana and Mali*
(London: Methuen, 1973).

5. The notion of empire as a composite put together by varied ties to a monarch was
propounded by John Elliott in regard to early-modern Europe. "A Europe of Composite
Monarchies," *Past and Present* 137 (1992): 48–71. The story of the making of Sunjiata's
empire has become an epic, still recounted centuries later. See D. T. Niane, *Sundiata:
An Epic of Old Mali,* rev. ed., trans. G. D. Pickett (London: Longman, 2006).

6. Michael Gomez, "Prequel as Sequel: Early West Africa and the Shape of Things
to Come," Unpublished paper, 2012. I am indebted to Professor Gomez for allowing
me to make use of this stimulating paper.

7. Levtzion, *Ancient Ghana and Mali,* 112.

8. Levtzion, 117, 122.

9. Nehimia Levtzion, "Islam in Bilad al-Sudan to 1800," in Levtzion and Randall
Powell, eds., *The History of Islam in Africa* (Athens: Ohio University Press, 2000),
68–69; Elias Saad, *Social History of Timbuktu: The Role of Muslims Scholars and Notables,
1400–1900* (Cambridge: Cambridge University Press, 1983).

10. Levtzion in Levtzion and Powell, 67–68.

11. The chronicles on which much of our knowledge of Sunni Ali is based por-
tray him as less than an ideal Muslim ruler, something of a "magician-king," who

combined Islamic and local religious rituals and practices in trying to sew together a complex empire. But as Lansiné Kaba points out, the portraits we have of him were written after the fact and reflect the viewpoint of his emperors who wanted to emphasize their own superior Islamic orientation. Hence, the chronicles' characterization of Sunni Ali should be taken with a grain of Saharan salt. "The Pen, the Sword, and the Crown: Islam and Revolution in Songhay Reconsidered, 1464–1493," *Journal of African History* 25 (1984): 241–56. For other views of the relationship of political authority and Islam in Songhay, see Michael Gomez, "Timbuktu under Imperial Songhay: A Reconsideration of Autonomy," *Journal of African History* 31 (1990): 5–24, and John Hunwick, "Secular Power and Religious Authority in Muslim Society: The Case of Songhay," *Journal of African History* 37 (1996): 175–94.

12. One of the leading experts on the Sudanese empires, P. F. De Moraes Farias, applies Jean-François Bayart's notion of extroversion (see Chapter 1) to these empires. *Arabic Medieval Inscriptions from the Republic of Mali: Epigraphy, Chronicles, and Songhay-Tuāreg History* (Oxford: Oxford University Press for the British Academy, 2003), cxvi.

13. Ivor Wilks, "Land, Labour, Capital, and the Forest Kingdom of Asante: A Model of Early Change," in J. Friedman and M. J. Rowlands, eds., *The Evolution of Social Systems* (Pittsburgh: University of Pittsburgh Press, 1978), 487–534.

14. The classic studies of Asante are Ivor Wilks, *Asante in the Nineteenth Century: The Structure and Evolution of a Political Order* (Cambridge: Cambridge University Press, 1989), and T. C. McCaskie, *State and Society in Pre-Colonial Asante* (Cambridge: Cambridge University Press, 1995). The biggest West African kingdoms differed in the extent to which they filled administrative roles by the extensive use of slaves (Oyo) or "free" subjects (Benin, Asante), but in either case the patrimonial principle—the ability of the king to choose and reward personal followers and to make himself the source of good fortune—was critical. See Robin Law, *The Oyo Empire, c.1600–c.1836: A West African Imperialism in the Era of the Atlantic Slave Trade* (Oxford: Clarendon Press, 1977), 308–12.

15. Mervyn Hiskett, *The Sword of Truth: The Life and Times of Shehu Usuman dan Fodio* (Evanston: Northwestern University Press, 1994); Murray Last, *The Sokoto Caliphate* (New York: Humanities Press, 1967); David Robinson, *The Holy War of Umar Tal* (Oxford: Oxford University Press, 1985); Yves Person, *Samori: une révolution dyula* (Dakar: IFAN, 1968).

16. Note the parallel, cited earlier in relation to Mali, with Elliott's concept of "composite monarchy" in Europe. "A Europe of Composite Monarchies."

17. John Wright, "Turbulent Times: Political Transformations in the North and East 1760s–1830s," in Carolyn Hamilton, Bernard Mbenga, and Robert Ross, eds, *Cambridge History of South Africa: Vol. 1, From Early Times to 1885* (Cambridge: Cambridge University Press, 2010), 211–52, 218 and 221 quoted. On debates over Zulu empire-building, see Carolyn Hamilton, ed., *The Mfecane Aftermath: Reconstructive Debates in*

Southern African History (Johannesburg: Witwatersrand University Press, 1995), and on myth-making, Carolyn Hamilton, *Terrific Majesty: The Power of Shaka Zulu and the Limits of Historical Invention* (Cambridge, MA: Harvard University Press, 1998).

18. As Jean-Pierre Chrétien and Hervé Pennec point out, it is all too easy to project a story of imperial continuity onto the entire history of Ethiopia. They emphasize the success of Menelik's empire-building but warn against reading it back onto a historical trajectory in which "multicentered monarchies" waxed and waned in different parts of the region, organizing themselves in different ways. But observers were particularly prone to projecting their fantasies onto Ethiopia's past. "Imaginaires et invention des empires. Afrique de l'Est: L'empire dans tous ses états," *Monde(s)* 2 (2012): 123–50, esp. 135–37. For an eloquent summary of recent Ethiopian history, see Bahru Zewde, *A History of Modern Ethiopia 1855–1991,* 2nd ed. (Athens: Ohio University Press, 2001).

19. Bruce Hall, *A History of Race in Muslim West Africa, 1600–1960* (Cambridge: Cambridge University Press, 2011), esp. 13, 41. Hall (52–53, 58) finds evidence of an increasing tendency after the Moroccan defeat of Songhay in 1591 of a discourse among desert elites that distinguished "blacks" from "Muslims," so much so that some Timbuktu scholars developed an argument against such an interpretation. He also discusses the importance of racial discourses in deciding who could be legitimately enslaved. For a related argument about a mid-twentieth-century instance of racialized conflict between people who divided themselves into "Arabs" and "Africans," see Jonathon Glassman, *War of Words, War of Stones: Racial Thought and Violence in Colonial Zanzibar* (Bloomington: Indiana University Press, 2011).

20. For an example of a *tu quo que* argument, see Bernard Lewis, *Race and Color in Islam* (New York: Harper, 1971). The thrust of his argument is to show that Muslims could be as racist as Europeans rather than to ask how Muslims, in particular historical situations, conceptualized, institutionalized, and reproduced invidious distinctions. The argument does not give us much precision about varying notions of distinction among Muslims.

21. J. F. Ade Ajayi, "The Continuity of African Institutions under Colonialism," in Terence O. Ranger, ed., *Emerging Themes of African History* (Nairobi: East African Publishing House, (1968), 189–200.

22. Both the usefulness and the limitations of this concept are evident in Achille Mbembe, *On the Postcolony* (Berkeley: University of California Press, 2001).

23. Frederick Cooper and Ann Laura Stoler, eds., *Tensions of Empire: Colonial Cultures in a Bourgeois World* (Berkeley: University of California Press, 1997).

24. This book went through many editions. Paul Leroy-Beaulieu, *De la colonisation chez les peuples modernes,* 6th ed. (Paris: Félix Alcan, 1908)

25. The eagerness of French officials to represent—to themselves as well as to a French public—their project as a civilizing mission followed by a move to less ambitious, less costly, less reformative policies is well described in Alice Conklin, *A Mission*

to Civilize: The Republican Idea of Empire in France and West Africa, 1895–1930 (Stanford: Stanford University Press, 1997).

26. Ronald Robinson and John Gallagher, "The Imperialism of Free Trade," Economic History Review 2nd series, 6 (1953): 1–15

27. This line of argument is developed in Burbank and Cooper, Empires in World History. See also Laura Doyle, "Inter-Imperiality: Dialectics in Postcolonial World History," Interventions 2013: 1–38.

28. K. O. Dike, Trade and Politics in the Niger Delta (Oxford: Oxford University Press, 1956).

29. Ewout Frankema, "Raising Revenue in the British Empire, 1870–1940: How 'extractive' were colonial taxes?" Journal of Global History 5 (2010): 447–477, 455, 466 cited.

30. A. H. M. Kirk-Greene, "The Thin White Line: The Size of the British Colonial Service in Africa," African Affairs 314 (1980): 25–44, 39 cited. The article enumerates 1223 administrators in Africa. Cambridge has about 3000 city employees. If one adds in medical personnel, military and police, and other specialized services, the number in British Africa comes to a little over 7,500—still a tiny number for such a vast space.

31. See for example Benjamin Lawrance, Emily Osborn, and Richard Roberts, eds., Intermediaries, Interpreters and Clerks: African Employees and the Making of Colonial Africa (Madison: University of Wisconsin Press, 2006).

32. On what Africans made of missionary stations and missionary teachings, see a growing literature, including Meredith McKittrick, To Dwell Secure: Generation, Christianity, and Colonialism in Ovamboland (Portsmouth: Heinemann, 2003); Derek Peterson, Creative Writing: Translation, Bookkeeping, and the Work of Imagination in Colonial Kenya (Portsmouth: Heinemann, 2004). On religious movements and a refusal to engage with colonial authority, see Karen Fields, Revival and Rebellion in Colonial Central Africa (Princeton: Princeton University Press, 1985).

33. For more on conceptual issues in the study of colonialism, see Frederick Cooper, Colonialism in Question: Theory, Knowledge, History (Berkeley: University of California Press, 2005).

34. Helen Tilley, Africa as a Living Laboratory: Empire, Development, and the Problem of Scientific Knowledge, 1870–1950 (Chicago: University of Chicago Press, 2011); Alice Conklin, In the Museum of Man: Race, Anthropology, and Empire in France, 1850–1950 (Ithaca: Cornell University Press, 2013).

35. Thomas Holt, The Problem of Freedom Race, Labor, and Politics in Jamaica and Britain, 1832–1938 (Baltimore: Johns Hopkins University Press, 1992); Catherine Hall, Civilising Subjects: Metropole and Colony in the English Imagination, 1830–1867 (Chicago: University of Chicago Press, 2002).

36. Ann Laura Stoler, Carnal Knowledge and Imperial Power: Race and the Intimate in Colonial Rule (Berkeley: University of California Press, 2002). For a different

perspective, see Emmanuelle Saada, *Empire's Children: Race, Filiation, and Citizenship in the French Colonies,* trans. Arthur Goldhammer (Chicago: University of Chicago Press, 2012).

37. Miguel Bandeira Jerónimo, "The 'Civilisation Guild': Race and Labour in the Third Portuguese Empire, c. 1870–1930," *Proceedings of the British Academy* 179 (2012): 173–99.

38. Frederick Cooper, "Conditions Analogous to Slavery: Imperialism and Free Labor Ideology in Africa," in Frederick Cooper, Thomas Holt, and Rebecca Scott, *Beyond Slavery: Explorations of Race, Labor, and Citizenship in Postemancipation Societies* (Chapel Hill: University of North Carolina Press, 2000), 107–50

39. J. E. Casely Hayford, *Gold Coast Native Institutions with Thoughts upon a Healthy Imperial Policy for the Gold Coast and Ashanti* (London: Cass, 1970 [1903]).

40. Ibid., 19.

41. Ibid., 254–55, 259.

42. Claude Liauzu, *Aux origines des tiers-mondismes: colonisés et anticolnialistes en France 1919–1939* (Paris: L'Harmattan, 1982); Jennifer Boittin, *Colonial Metropolis: The Urban Grounds of Anti-Imperialism and Feminism in Interwar Paris* (Omaha: University of Nebraska Press, 2010); Harald Fischer-Tiné, "Indian Nationalism and the 'World Forces': Transnational and Diasporic Dimensions of the Indian Freedom Movement on the Eve of the First World War," *Journal of Global History* 2 (2007): 325–44; Erez Manela, *The Wilsonian Moment: Self-determination and the International Origins of Anticolonial Nationalism* (New York: Oxford University Press, 2007).

43. Moses Ochonu, *Colonial Meltdown: Northern Nigeria in the Great Depression* (Athens: Ohio University Press, 2009).

44. The Manchester conference resolutions are reprinted in J. Ayodele Langley, ed., *Ideologies of Liberation in Black Africa, 1856–1970: Documents on Modern African Political Thought from Colonial Times to the Present* (London: Collings, 1979), 758–61.

45. What follows is largely based on my "Decolonization and Citizenship: Africa between Empire and a World of Nations," in Els Bogaerts and Remco Raben, eds., *Beyond Empire and Nation: The Decolonization of African and Asian Societies, 1930s–1960s* (Leiden: KITLV Press, 2012), 39–68. For an argument situating the decolonization of Africa in a longer history of empires, see Burbank and Cooper, *Empires in World History,* Chapter 13.

46. Ministre de la France d'Outre-Mer, circular to Haut Commissaires, Commissaires, Gouverneurs, et Chefs de Territoire, 15 December 1947, 17G 152, Archives du Sénégal.

47. Tilley, *Africa as a Living Laboratory.*

48. For changing iterations of race thinking, see Thomas Holt, *The Problem of Race in the Twenty-first Century* (Cambridge, MA: Harvard University Press, 2000).

49. Frederick Cooper, "Mau Mau and the Discourses of Decolonization: Review Article," *Journal of African History* 29 (1988): 313–20; Todd Shepard, *The Invention of*

Decolonization: The Algerian War and the Remaking of France (Ithaca: Cornell University Press, 2006).

50. Kwame Nkrumah, *Ghana: The Autobiography of Kwame Nkrumah* (New York: Nelson, 1957).

51. Frantz Fanon, *The Wretched of the Earth,* trans. Constance Farrington (New York: Grove Press, 1963 [original 1961]).

52. Jean Marie Allman, *The Quills of the Porcupine: Asante Nationalism in an Emergent Ghana* (Madison: University of Wisconsin Press, 1993).

53. Du Bois's speech is reprinted as an appendix to the International Publisher's edition of *World and Africa,* 305–10, 309 quoted.

3. Africa and the Nation-State

1. This chapter draws on my own archival research far more than the previous ones. A much fuller analysis appears in *Citizenship between Empire and Nation: Remaking France and French Africa, 1945–1960* (Princeton: Princeton University Press, 2014).

2. D. Bruce Marshall, *The French Colonial Myth and Constitution Making in the Fourth Republic* (New Haven: Yale University Press, 1973).

3. Partha Chatterjee has argued that nationalists' embrace of the nation-state was itself derivative from Europe. *Nationalist Thought and the Colonial World: A Derivative Discourse?* (London: Zed, 1986).

4. Benjamin Stora points out that it was difficult to give a face to the Algerian revolution because there were so many purges and violent conflicts among its leadership. *La Gangrène et l'oubli: la mémoire de la guerre d'Algérie* (Paris, La Découverte, 2005). See also Martin Evans and John Phillips, *Algeria: Anger of the Dispossessed* (New Haven: Yale University Press, 2007).

5. *La Condition Humaine,* 29 August 1955.

6. See the autobiography of Mamadou Dia, *Mémoires d'un militant du tiers-monde* (Paris: Publisud, 1985).

7. One of the best studies of the mutual effacing of memory of the complex politics in the years before independence is Stora, *La gangrène et l'oubli.*

8. Several political leaders from both European and African France in the late 1940s and 1950s argued for the notion of "Eurafrique"—in which France's African territories would be included in the effort to integrate France with other countries of Europe. African leaders insisted that they should have a voice in the governance of any such entity. By 1957, it was becoming clear that most of France's European partners would not accept the consequences of including its African territories within a European common market. Yves Montarsolo, *L'Eurafrique contrepoint de l'idée de l'Europe: Le cas français de la fin de la deuième guerre mondiale aux négociations des Traités de Rome* (Aix-en-Provence: Publications de l'Université de Provence, 2010); Marie-Thérèse Bitsch

and Gérard Bossuat, eds., *L'Europe unie et l'Afrique: de l'idée d'Eurafrique à la convention de Lomé I* (Brussels: Bruylant, 2005).

9. For an empire-wide perspective in these issues, see Emmanuelle Saada, *Empire's Children: Race, Filiation, and Citizenship in the French Colonies,* trans. Arthur Goldhammer (Chicago: University of Chicago Press, 2012).

10. Mamadou Diouf, "The French Colonial Policy of Assimilation and the Civility of the Originaires of the Four Communes (Senegal): A Nineteenth Century Globalization Project," *Development and Change* 29 (1998): 671–96.

11. Assemblée Nationale Constituante, Rapport Supplementaire of Commission de la Constitution, Léopold Senghor, reporter, 5 April 1946, in Assemblée Nationale Constituante, *Documents,* Report #885. His oral presentation to the Assemblée made similar points. Assemblée Nationale Constituante, *Débats,* 11 April 1946, 1713–15.

12. For the text of the constitution, see http://www.conseil-constitutionnel.fr /conseil-constitutionnel/francais/la-constitution/les-constitutions-de-la-france /constitution-de-1946-IVe-republique.5109.html. The debates are treated in detail in my *Citizenship between Empire and Nation.*

13. AOF, Directeur Général des Affaires Politiques, Administratives et Sociales (Berlan), note, July 46, 17G 152, Archives du Sénégal.

14. Senghor used these expressions repeatedly. A particularly clear expression of them is in his political party's newspaper, *La Condition Humaine,* 11 July 1948.

15. Senghor, "Rapport sur le méthode du Parti," to Congress of BDS, 15–17 April 1949, *La Condition Humaine,* 26 April 1949.

16. Léopold Senghor, "Les Négro-Africains et l'Union Française," *Réveil,* 24 April 1947.

17. "Déclaration du groupe interparlementaire des Indépendants d'Outre-Mer (24 Décembre 1948)," and "Situation des Indépendants d'outre-mer en 1950," copies in AP 2257/3, Archives d'Outre-Mer, Aix-en-Provence; statements of the political parties, in Assemblée Nationale, *Débats,* 6 July 1951, 5909; *La Condition Humaine,* 25 February 1953.

18. Manifesto reproduced in Joseph Roger de Benoist, *L'Afrique Occidentale Française de 1944 à 1960* (Dakar: Nouvelles Editions Africaines, 1982, 559–61; *Réveil,* 30 September 1946.

19. See the excellent biography of Senghor, Janet Vaillant, *Black, French, and African: A Life of Léopold Sédar Senghor* (Cambridge, MA: Harvard University Press, 1990).

20. Frederick Cooper, "Conditions Analogous to Slavery: Imperialism and Free Labor Ideology in Africa," in Frederick Cooper, Thomas Holt, and Rebecca Scott, *Beyond Slavery: Explorations of Race, Labor, and Citizenship in Postemancipation Societies* (Chapel Hill: University of North Carolina Press, 2000), 107–50; Aristide Zolberg, *One-party Government in the Ivory Coast* (Princeton: Princeton University Press, 1969).

21. Elizabeth Schmidt, *Mobilizing the Masses: Gender, Ethnicity, and Class in the Nationalist Movement in Guinea, 1939–1958* (Portsmouth: Heinemann, 2005). On Sékou Touré's shift from class struggle to African unity, see Frederick Cooper, *Decolonization and African Society: The Labor Question in French and British Africa* (Cambridge: Cambridge University Press, 1996), 415–18.

22. In the first election under the constitution, in November 1946, just under 800,000 people in French West Africa were counted as legal voters, out of a population of perhaps fifteen million. About three million voters were registered by June 1951, rising to six million by January 1956. It was only then that universal suffrage was put in place, and by early 1957, ten million people were on the rolls, more than half of the population. De Benoist, *L'Afrique Occidentale* Française, 513.

23. Frederick Cooper, "The Senegalese General Strike of 1946 and the Labor Question in Post-War French Africa," *Canadian Journal of African Studies* 24 (1990): 165–215; Frederick Cooper, " 'Our Strike': Equality, Anticolonial Politics, and the French West African Railway Strike of 1947–48," *Journal of African History* 37 (1996): 81–118.

24. Cooper, *Decolonization and African Society,* Chapters 10 and 11.

25. Jacques Tronchon, *L'insurrection malgache de 1947: essai d'interprétation historique* (Paris: Maspero, 1974); Raphaëlle Branche, *La torture et l'armée pendant la guerre d'Algérie 1954–1962* (Paris: Gallimard, 2001); Richard Joseph, *Radical Nationalism in Cameroun: The Social Origins of the UPC Rebellion* (Oxford: Oxford University Press, 1977); Achille Mbembe, *La Naissance du maquis dans le Sud-Cameroun, 1920–1960: Histoire des usages de la raison en colonie* (Paris: Karthala, 1996).

26. Todd Shepard, *The Invention of Decolonization: The Algerian War and the Remaking of France* (Ithaca: Cornell University Press, 2006).

27. These incidents are discussed in my *Citizenship between Empire and Nation*. See also Ruth Schachter Mogenthau, *Political Parties in French-Speaking West Africa* (Oxford: Clarendon, 1964), 188–202.

28. "Discours d'ouverture du President Mamadou Dia au premier seminaire national d'études pour les responsables politiques, parlementaires, gouvernementaux," 26 October 1959, "Sur la construction nationale," VP 93, Archives du Sénégal.

29. *L'Afrique Nouvelle,* 1 October 1957, 7 March 1958.

30. *Abidjan-Matin,* 5, 17 September 1959.

31. Klaas van Walraven, "Decolonization by Referendum: The Anomaly of Niger and the Fall of Sawaba, 1958–1959," *Journal of African History* 50 (2009): 269–92.

32. Elizabeth Schmidt, "Anticolonial Nationalism in French West Africa: What Made Guinea Unique?" *African Studies Review* 52 (2009): 1–34.

33. "Discours d'ouverture du President Mamadou Dia," VP 93, Archives du Sénégal.

34. On this episode, see my " 'Une nationalité superposée': Being French and African in 1959," *Maghreb et Sciences Sociales* (2012), 133–44.

35. Telegrams, labeled very secret, from Haut Commissaire, Dakar, to President of Community, 8, 17 December 1959, FPR 231, 5AG, Archives Nationales de France.

36. Guédel Ndiaye, *L'échec de la fédération du Mali* (Dakar: Nouvelles éditions africaines, 1980), 103–118; William Foltz, *From French West Africa to the Mali Federation* (New Haven: Yale University Press, 1965); Alain Gandolfi, "Naissance et mort sur le plan international d'un Etat éphémère: La Fédération du Mali," *Annuaire français du droit international* 6 (1960): 880–906.

37. Report of David Soumah, Secretary General, to Congrès de la CATC, Abidjan, 10–12 March 1958, 17G 610, Archives du Sénégal. See also Claude Rivière, "Lutte ouvrière et phénomène syndical en guinée," *Cultures et Développement* 7 (1975): 53–83.

38. For Houphouët-Boigny's resentment and its relationship to his demand for independence, see his statements reported in the Ivorian press, *Abidjan-Matin,* 7 June 1960, and *Fraternité,* 10 June 1960.

39. Henri-Michel Yéré, "Citizenship, Nationality & History in Côte d'Ivoire, 1929–1999," Ph.D. dissertation, University of Basel, 2010.

40. Edward J. Schumacher, *Politics, Bureaucracy and Rural Development in Senegal* (Berkeley: University of California Press, 1975), 63–67; Catherine Boone, *Merchant Capital and the Roots of State Power in Senegal 1930–1985* (New York: Cambridge University Press, 1992), 91–94; Mamadou Diouf, "Le clientélisme, la 'technocratie' et après?" in Momar-Coumba Diop, ed., *Sénégal: Trajectoires d'un Etat* (Dakar: Codesria, 1992), 250–52. Dia's version is in *Memoires,* 143–75.

41. Bruce Hall, *A History of Race in Muslim West Africa, 1600–1960* (Cambridge: Cambridge University Press, 2011). See the discussion of race in African empires in Chapter 2.

42. For ongoing discussions of the Mali situation, see africanarguments.org, especially a conversation among Bruce Hall, Gregory Mann, Baz Lecoq, and Bruce Whitehouse, May 14, 2013, accessed June 18, 2013.

43. Senghor's view of state and nation was set out most clearly in Léopold Senghor, "Pour une solution fédéraliste," *La Nef* Cahier 9 (June 1955), 148–61. For another critical perspective on the hyphenated expression, see Basil Davidson, *The Black Man's Burden: Africa and the Curse of the Nation-State* (New York, 1992). There is, however, an anti-state argument prevalent in certain quarters of western social science, for example in James Scott, *Seeing Like a State: How Certain Schemes to Improve the Human Condition Have Failed* (New Haven: Yale University Press, 1998). Anyone considering variations on this theme should think long and hard about what life without a functioning state actually means in today's world, especially the examples of northern Mali and Somalia.

44. Senegal has also had a secession problem that persisted over decades in the region of Casamance, separated for the most part from the rest of Senegal by the anglophone state of Gambia (see map 4). In the early 1950s, Senghor partly succeeded

in getting the major Casamance political party to affiliate with his own party, but as power became closer Senghor and Dia's desire for a more unified party structure gave less and less space for such layered arrangements. Violent conflict in the region has waxed and waned. See the essay of Séverine Awenengo Dalberto in *Frontières et indépendances en Afrique,* forthcoming.

Conclusion

1. Matthew Wendeln, "Contested Territory: Regional Development in France 1934–1968," dissertation for joint doctoral program, Ecole des Hautes Etudes en Sciences Sociales and New York University, 2011.

2. For some time there has been a debate among economists who see foreign aid as a necessary component of economic progress—given the lack of alternatives—and those who see it as precluding accountability for economic policies and as sustaining corrupt and inefficient regimes. But the entire debate is framed by a presumption of neat and unquestioned separation between states and between people. For the two sides of the current debate, see Jeffrey Sachs, *The End of Poverty: Economic Possibilities for Our Time* (New York: Penguin, 2005), and William Easterly, *The White Man's Burden: Why the West's Efforts to Aid the Rest Have Done So Much Ill and So Little Good* (New York: Penguin, 2006).

3. The best scholarship on sovereignty recognizes that it is a bundle of claims, separable and variable, as opposed to a model of sovereign states as billiard balls, solid in themselves and bouncing off each other in an international arena, a model often projected, wrongly, to the Westphalian treaties of 1648. For a concise and eloquent analysis, see James J. Sheehan, "The Problem of Sovereignty in European History," *American Historical Review* 111 (2006): 1–15, and for a discussion of sovereignty looking from an ambiguous past to a complex future, see Jean L. Cohen, *Globalization and Sovereignty: Rethinking Legality, Legitimacy, and Constitutionalism* (Cambridge: Cambridge University Press, 2012).

4. Alain Supiot, *The Spirit of Philadelphia: Social Justice Vs. The Total Market,* trans. Saskia Brown (London: Verso, 2012).

5. I have discussed these issues at greater length in "Social Rights and Human Rights in the Time of Decolonization," *Humanity: An International Journal of Human Rights, Humanitarianism, and Development* 3, no. 3 (2012): 473–92. See also Roland Burke, *Decolonization and the Evolution of International Human Rights* (Philadelphia: University of Pennsylvania Press, 2010).

6. François Manchuelle, *Willing Migrants: Soninke Labor Diasporas, 1848–1960* (Athens: Ohio University Press, 1997).

7. The decidedly mixed record of the administration of metropolitan France in respecting the rights of overseas citizens (especially those from Algeria) is clear from

Alexis Spire, *Etrangers à la carte: L'administration de l'immigration en France (1945–1975)* (Paris: Grasset, 2005), Chapter 6.

8. Kathleen Paul, *Whitewashing Britain: Race and Citizenship in the Postwar Era* (Ithaca: Cornell University Press, 1997).

9. Sylvain Laurens, " '1974' et la fermature des frontières: Analyse critique d'une décision érigée en *turning point*," *Politix* 21, 82 (2008): 69–94; Paul, *Whitewashing Britain*.

10. Hervé Le Bras, *L'invention de l'immigré* (Paris: L'Aube, 2012); Patrick Weil, *Qu'est ce qu'un Français? Histoire de la nationalité française depuis la Révolution* (Paris: Grasset, 2002).

11. Senghor to Assemblée ad hoc chargé d'élaborer un projet de Traité instituant une Communauté Politiqiue Européene, Strasbourg, 8–9 January 1953, AP 219/3, Archives d'Outre-Mer, Aix-en-Provence.

12. Ministre des Affaires Economiques to Ministre de la France d'Outre-Mer, 3 August 1956, Ministère de la France d'Outre-Mer, "Note au sujet du projet 'Euratom'," 2 February 1956, and Ministre to Président du Conseil, 3 April 1956, AP 2316/5, Archives d'Outre-Mer.

13. Guia Migani, *La France et l'Afrique sub-saharienne, 1957–1963: Histoire d'une décolonisation entre idéaux eurafricains et politique de puissance* (Brussels: PIE Peter Lang, 2008).

14. Lauren MacLean, *Informal Institutions and Citizenship in Rural Africa: Risk and Reciprocity in Ghana and Côte d'Ivoire* (Cambridge: Cambridge University Press, 2010).

15. On this sequence, see Frederick Cooper, *Africa since 1940: The Past of the Present* (Cambridge: Cambridge University Press, 2002). A more detailed study of the post-independence period is Paul Nugent, *Africa since Independence: A Comparative History* (Blasingstoke: Palgrave-Macmillan, 2012).

16. Stephen Ellis, *Season of Rains: Africa in the World* (Chicago: University of Chicago Press, 2012), 55.

17. For a particularly detailed study of how a government, over many years, used a combination of repression and patronage to prevent any challenge to its authority—under both one-party and multi-party electoral regimes—see Daniel Branch, *Kenya: Between Hope and Despair, 1963–2012* (New Haven: Yale University Press, 2012).

18. Jean-Pierre Bat, *Le syndrome Foccart: La politique française en Afrique, de 1959 à nos jours* (Paris: Gallimard, 2012).

Index

Abubakari II, 45
Acemoglu, Daron, 31
Africa, historical interpretations of, 1, 5, 7, 8–10, 32, 41, 51, 54, 66, 69
African Americans, 4–5, 57, 103–104n3
African societies: adaptability of, 11, 14, 17, 23–24, 27, 30, 33, 36, 43–44, 52; alleged backwardness of, 11, 14, 20, 25–27, 29, 36–37, 39, 58, 62, 73, 90; and cultural change, 7, 22, 43, 45, 51, 54, 55, 59, 75; and global interdependence, 7–8, 10, 13–14, 32, 34–37, 44–47, 75–76, 90–92, 98, 99–101; and resistance to capitalism, 14, 18, 21, 30, 33, 36
African unity, 60, 64, 81–82, 84
Afrique Occidentale Française (AOF). *See* French West Africa
agriculture: in African empires, 43, 47; African initiative in, 1, 22, 24–25, 35, 54; and colonization, 22–26, 54; and New World crops, 18. *See also* cocoa; coffee; development; settlers; sugar
Ajayi, Jacob, 51
Akan, 97
Algeria, 27, 62, 68, 70, 72, 78, 87
All Africa Peoples Conference, 64
Al Qaeda in the Islamic Maghreb, 87–88

amabutho, 49
Angola, 17, 30, 34, 68
anticolonial politics: alternative forms of, 6–8, 57, 59, 62–65, 66–83, 91, 101; and claims for social equality, 5–6, 27, 31, 60, 62, 72–78, 80, 93–94. *See also* nationalism
antislavery movements, 5–6, 19–20, 30, 52, 57
Antilles. *See* Caribbean
apartheid, 28, 30, 31
apprenticeship, 20
Aro, 17
Asante, 38, 47–48, 57–58, 64
Asia, 13, 32, 47, 59, 60–61, 100
Assemblée Nationale Constituante, 7, 71–73, 77
assimilation, 7, 40
association, 59
Atlantic Charter, 4, 60
Atlantic Ocean, 15–17, 45, 47, 88
Australia, 94
Azawad, 87, 89

"balkanization," 69, 79–80, 83, 86
Bandung, 64
Bayart, Jean-François, 21
Belgian Congo, 21, 22, 55, 57

nation: ambiguity of concept of, 8, 64, 65,
69–70, 82, 85, 89, 91, 96; and European
Union, 95–96. *See also* confederation;
federation; state, post-colonial
nationalism, 35, 65, 69, 75, 76
nationality, 74, 82, 94
Nationality Act (Great Britain), 94
nation-state, 3, 8, 39–40, 65, 66–89, 91, 96,
99–100
Nazis, 4
Ndebele, 49
Negro-African civilization, 63, 75, 89
neo-colonialism, 9, 28–29, 92
Netherlands. *See* Dutch
New Christians, 16
Niger, 35, 82, 84, 96
Niger Delta, 14, 54
Nigeria, 8, 17, 22, 25, 27, 54, 55
Niger River, 42, 43
Nkrumah, Kwame, 6, 8, 62–65
North Africa, 15, 43, 44
North America, 12, 100
Nwokeji, G. Ugo, 17

oil, 29, 30, 34, 100
Ottoman Empire, 13, 15, 40, 47, 53
Ouattara, Alessane, 85
Oyo, 114n14

Pakistan, 60
palm oil, 18, 53, 54
Pan-Africanism, 3, 6–7, 59–60, 62
Parthasarathi, Prasannan, 11–13
Parti Démocratique de la Côte d'Ivoire
(PDCI-RDA), 77
patron-client relations, 24, 30–31, 34, 96,
98–100
peasants, 19, 21–22, 27, 45
Philippines, 60
plantations, 5–6, 11–13, 25
political parties: in British West Africa, 58;
and single-party regimes, 86; social basis
of, 77; strength of, 81–82; territorial basis
of, 79, 82–83, 87. *See also* Bloc Démocratique
Sénégalais; Mouvement des Indépendants
d'Outre-Mer; Rassemblement Démocratique
Africain; Union des Populations du
Cameroun
Pomeranz, Kenneth, 11–13

population, 14–15, 42
ports, 4, 16–27, 22, 26–27, 54, 55, 60
Portugal, 15–17, 21, 43, 47, 49, 57
postcolony, 52. *See also* state, post-colonial
poverty, 4, 7, 11, 14, 29–30, 34, 74, 84
power, unevenness of, 9–10, 34, 36,
46, 91
primitive accumulation, 19, 21

Qadaffi, Moumar, 87
Qing Dynasty, 13
Quatre Communes,72, 76

race: and colonialism, 3, 39, 55–57; contested views of, 56–57; in Du Bois's writing, 38–39, 56, 57; mixing, 16, 56, 72; and
post–World War II era, 39, 60–62, 74, 75,
94; in Sahel, 50–51, 87; and science, 56,
61; in South Africa, 21–22, 28, 31
railroads, 22–23, 27, 78
Rassemblement Démocratique Africain
(RDA), 76, 79
Rhodesia, 22
Robinson, James, 31
Roman Empire, 40, 53, 74

SADCC (Southern African Development
Cooperation Conference), 100
Sahara Desert, 15, 43–44, 46, 87–88
Sahel, 15, 43–47
Saint-Domingue, 5–6, 71–72
Samori, 48
sans-papiers, 95
scholars: and Africa, 3, 8, 9, 11, 39,
49, 50–52, 55, 56; Islamic, 45–46,
115n19
scramble for Africa, 53–54
segregation, 28
Sékou Touré, 77, 80–84
self-determination, 27, 39, 59, 64
self-government, 4, 6, 58, 79
Senegal, 7, 62, 63, 68–69, 71, 72, 75–80, 82,
85–86, 89, 91, 96, 99
Senegambia, 15–16
Senghor, Léopold Sédar, 63–65, 68–69,
72–77, 83, 85–86, 89, 95, 96, 100
settlers, 21–22, 50, 55, 62, 72
Shaka, 49
Sierra Leone, 34